Six Steps to Preparing Exemplary Principals and Superintendents

Leadership Education at Its Best

John R. Hoyle and Mario S. Torres, Jr.

Rowman & Littlefield Education
A division of
ROWMAN & LITTLEFIELD PUBLISHERS, INC.
Lanham • New York • Toronto • Plymouth, UK

Published by Rowman & Littlefield Education
A division of Rowman & Littlefield Publishers, Inc.
A wholly owned subsidiary of The Rowman & Littlefield Publishing Group, Inc.
4501 Forbes Boulevard, Suite 200, Lanham, Maryland 20706
http://www.rowmaneducation.com

Estover Road, Plymouth PL6 7PY, United Kingdom

British Library Cataloguing in Publication Information Available

Library of Congress Cataloging-in-Publication Data

Hoyle, John R.
Six steps to preparing exemplary principals and superintendents : leadership education at its best / John R. Hoyle and Mario S. Torres, Jr.
p. cm.
Includes bibliographical references and index.
ISBN 978-1-60709-686-3 (cloth : alk. paper) — ISBN 978-1-60709-687-0 (pbk. : alk. paper) — ISBN 978-1-60709-688-7 (electronic)
1. School principals—United States. 2. School superintendents—United States. 3. School supervision—United States. 4. School administration—United States. I. Torres, Mario S. II. Title.
LB2831.92.H72 2010
371.20071'1—dc22

2009048165

™ The paper used in this publication meets the minimum requirements of American National Standard for Information Sciences—Permanence of Paper for Printed Library Materials, ANSI/NISO Z39.48-1992.

Printed in the United States of America

Contents

Preface

This book is written out of respect for the legions of former and current professors of educational administration who have prepared thousands of dedicated and skilled school leaders. Since the twentieth century, our colleagues have sought to improve the selection, preparation, and continued professional development of their students and the schools they serve. As the old Texas farmer said, "We ain't where we wanna' be, and we ain't where were gonna' be, but we ain't where we wuz." Our leadership education programs across the United States and Canada have made quantum leaps in improving the research, teaching, and collaborations with school administrators, board members, legislators, and communities to prepare leaders for all children and youth. As the amazing Renaissance artist Michelangelo created David, arguably the world's most riveting masterpiece, by chipping him out of a block of marble, we in leadership education strive to 'chip' away everything that does not emerge as a great school leader.

While critical analysis of our professional performance challenges us to improve, we also realize that much of the criticism comes from individual and well-funded foundation reports that fail to provide suggestions for improvement in leadership education programs. This book provides suggestions for program improvement derived from research and from colleagues that scrutinize the links between preparation and successful practices of graduates now serving as principals and superintendents and in other leadership roles.

We implore our colleagues in universities and others engaged in administrator preparation and licensure to read our work. We have collected the latest research about and best practices for selecting excellent candidates for school leadership, pretesting candidates to determine their entry level knowledge and skills, and creating curricula that assure all students not only pass ISLLC and other licensure examinations but also achieve the highest levels of knowledge for leading schools and communities to excellence in public education. The reader will also find advice on structuring graduate advisory committees that hold high standards for each other and the student, followed by the importance of maintaining a talented and caring office support staff that improves communications among the office personnel, students, and staff. Finally, we suggest best practices and model questionnaires for assessing the quality of programs through the eyes of current and former students.

We are proud of our professional discipline of educational administration and the critical role we play in selecting and preparing the excellent school leaders our children and youth deserve.

About the Authors

John R. Hoyle, PhD, is senior professor of educational administration and future studies at Texas A&M University. He received the first NCPEA Living Legend Award and was selected in a national survey as one of four "Exceptional Living Scholars" in educational administration/leadership. He has authored or coauthored twelve books, over one hundred book chapters and refereed articles and has supervised 120 dissertations. He writes in the areas of leadership education, servant leadership, organizational theory, leadership and visioning, and leading with love.

Mario S. Torres, Jr. is an assistant professor in educational administration at Texas A&M University. Prior to his faculty appointment, Dr. Torres worked as a middle school teacher in the San Antonio Independent School District where he served in various leadership roles. His scholarly interests include education law, administrative discretion, politics, and policy. He has published in the field's premier journals including the *Educational Administration Quarterly*, *Journal of Educational Administration*, and *Education and Urban Society*. He is currently a research fellow with the Mexican American and U.S. Latino Research Center.

Acknowledgments

We wish to thank our National Council of Professors of Educational Administation and University Council for Educational Administation colleagues who attended our general and invited sessions and encouraged us to write this book. We thank Linda Morford, 2007 president of NCPEA, and Michelle Young, executive director of UCEA, for invitations to present our research on a national stage. Our presentations counteracted some of the criticism about whether our leadership education programs and professors could produce graduates who actually lead schools and school districts to higher performance. We produced evidence that graduates from university leadership education programs are taught the skills and knowledge to improve school and student performance. However, more research and best practices are needed to keep improving the art and science of our work. The encouragement from our colleagues to produce a book was followed by an invitation by Thomas Koerner, a long time colleague with Rowman & Littlefield Education, to produce this manuscript. We hope this book will help guide our respected colleagues in improving or beginning new programs in educational administration. Also, we wish to thank Carolyn Hoyle for her excellent editing and Helyde Torres and children Sergio and Evelyn for their patience and encouragement to complete this book in the midst of many other demands. Finally, many thanks go to Maera Stratton, Assistant Editor, Rowman & Littlefield Education. Her patience and expertise helped this work become a reality.

John R. Hoyle and Mario Torres, Jr.

Acronyms

AASA	American Association of School Administrators
CCSSO	Council of Chief State School Officers
CSA	Clinical Scientist Associate program
DCQ	Doctoral Cohort Questionnaire
EDAD	Educational Administration
ELLC	Educational Leadership Constituent Council
GPR	Grade Point Ratio
GRE	Graduate Record Examination
IDPEL	Doctoral Program for Educational Leaders
IELTS	International English Language Testing System
IRB	Institutional Review Board
ISLLC	Interstate School Leaders Licensure Consortium
LSI	Leadership Skills Inventory
MAT	Miller Analogies Test
McREL	Mid-continent Research for Education and Learning
MELAB	Michigan English Language Battery
NAESP	National Association for Elementary School Principals
NASSP	National Association of Secondary School Principals
NCATE	National Council for Accreditation of Teacher Education
NCEEA	National Commission on Excellence in Educational Administration
NCES	National Center for Education Statistics
NCPEA	National Council of Professors of Educational Administration
NEA	National Endowment for the Arts
NPBEA	National Policy Board for Educational Administrators

PSM	Professional Studies Model
SLPPS	School Leadership Preparation and Practice Survey
TOEFL	Test of English as a Foreign Language
TTVN	Trans-Texas Video Conference Network
UCEA	University Council for Educational Administration

1

The Ground Floor

Now is the time to produce the kind of school leaders our children deserve. Criticism continues about the selection of candidates, relevance of what is taught, how it is taught, and the silent or fragile research links between what is taught and its impact on graduates becoming successful school principals and superintendents. This book begins with the ground floor of our field that includes some of the history and struggle to create a solid knowledge base and prepare exemplary principals and superintendents.

Leading up from the ground floor are six steps built with the strongest planks and newest handrails in our discipline. These steps may spark new energies and ideas despite cacophonous criticism and enervate professors in educational administration to shape exemplary preparation for a new generation of school leaders. Critics suggest that we have an overabundance of degree-granting programs, many of which are offered at non-research-intensive institutions, and that these programs are diminishing the quality of leadership education. However, most critics are not professors and mentors working to improve the process but are distant observers with limited data and ample foundation dollars.

Also, some reformers claim to have the answers to improving the talent pool of school principals. New York City Schools Chancellor Joel I. Klein helped create the New York City Leadership Academy to train young graduates of top colleges to become school principals (Gootman & Gebeloff 2009). According to Klein, "I wanted to change the old system. New leadership is a powerful way to do that" (1).

However, an analysis by the *New York Times* shows that schools led by younger Leadership Academy graduates have not done as well as those led by experienced principals or new principals prepared in traditional leadership education graduate programs. Findings report that schools led by Leadership Academy graduates had higher teacher turnover than schools led by older, more experienced principals.

Thus, professors in traditional leadership education programs glance at the critical reform efforts and proclaim that their leadership education programs are superior to alternative licensure or training programs and are seeking evidence to support their claims. However, perplexing questions go unanswered about the most productive ways to select and prepare new school leaders. Why do some graduates with leadership potential never succeed and others with what appears to be limited potential accomplish great things?

Why do we struggle in attracting and educating the United States' best to lead our schools? These unanswered questions about program quality have given rise to alternative leadership preparation academies similar to the one in New York City. According to Dick Flanary (2009) at the National Association of Secondary School Principals, there is a growing debate about the effectiveness of leadership academies and traditional university and college principal preparation programs. Flanary claims that "In part, those academies are reactionary in response to programs at traditional colleges and universities, as there is a real gap between principal preparation and principal readiness" (3).

Rosemary Papa and Ric Brown (2007) concur with Flanary that the gap between preparation and readiness continues. They believe it is essential that the professional doctorate in educational administration/leadership contain clear goals, rigorous standards, and serve potential, current, and former students, school districts, and participating faculty. Thus, this book is written to present relevant research and best practices in creating and improving traditional or alternative leadership education programs for principals and superintendents.

THE TALENT POOL FOR SCHOOL LEADERS

The struggle to attract larger numbers of the best candidates for administrative careers in public education is compounded by the prediction that more than 40 percent of the nation's 93,000 principals plan to retire in the next five to six years (Guterman 2009), and 82 percent of the 14,300 superintendents in the United States have reached retirement age (Danitz 2009).

Political pressure on principals and superintendents has intensified with "high stakes testing" and related No Child Left Behind requirements. Research indicates that the high stakes movement has helped identify the learning gaps in children of color and poverty who were among the forgotten failures of the past (Lunenburg 2002). However, others claim that these testing pressures and unfunded mandates have created collateral damage resulting in lower morale, high teacher turnover, breeches in testing ethics, and little improvement in student dropouts (Nichols & Berliner 2007).

Thus, these growing pressures on educators help explain why fewer young stars are attracted to administrative positions in public education. Also, the compensation for principals is not that attractive. The difference in salary between a senior teacher and a principal can be approximately $30,000, but on an hourly basis, that is only $2.00 more (Guterman 2009).

Although the average salary for superintendents is around $170,000 and over $200,000 for those in urban districts, money is only one factor that encourages them to stay. Superintendents last approximately seven years in suburban or rural districts but only two and a half years in urban jobs. The job of urban superintendent is extremely demanding and stressful. Bruce Cooper, a scholar at Fordham University, says, "If you make God New York City Chancellor, She wouldn't succeed. Everyone is second guessing you, from the mayor, to the city council, to the teachers, to the parents" (Danitz 2009, 1).

Along with the salary and stress issues that diminish the attractiveness of the roles of principal or superintendent, professors struggle to understand why some graduates succeed and others fail. Research provides few clues as to why some graduates who become school administrators adjust to change and stress better than others and why some are more reflective and gregarious than others. Also, some graduates have an inner sense of when and how to act under pressure, while others fail to act or lose their composure.

Perhaps the greatest barrier to systematic improvement is the limited research about leadership education programs' actual impact on successful on-the-job performance of their graduates. However, a study of six of the *U.S. News and World Report* top-ranked educational administration programs revealed that principals and superintendents in higher performing schools and school districts gave credit for their leadership success to the quality of their experiences in doctoral programs and to their professors (Hoyle & Torres 2008).

Another ongoing project, *School Leadership Preparation and Practice Survey* (*SLPPS*; 2009), is an online survey designed to solicit feedback from graduates and alumni about their leadership preparation and has sought data on graduates' leadership practices and the impact of these practices on school improvement work and school outcomes. Thus far the *SLPPS* data reconfirm previous research on the common characteristics and behaviors of successful school leaders, but currently little data link those behaviors to actual school and student performance.

Professors are challenged to improve leadership education by selecting a talented, diverse pool of students, conducting quality research, and seeking the best practices to guide programs through winds of bureaucratic challenge and change. Therefore, the six steps detailed in this book are designed to provide answers to help chart that successful course.

To establish the context for the six steps, the authors of this book begin with a brief description of the historical development of the leadership education field since the 1950s, highlighting the struggle to find tighter links between preparation and successful practice. Other key topics address enduring disagreements about whether educational administration is an applied science or skilled craft, issues around standards-based curriculum, the delicate balance between online and face-to-face delivery of content and academic rigor. Next is the thrust of the book—six practical steps to preparing exemplary principals and superintendents in both master's and doctoral leadership education programs.

WINDS OF CHANGE IN LEADERSHIP EDUCATION

Since the early 1900s scholars have recorded the winds of change in leadership education (Cubberly 1927; Culbertson 1988). The college-level courses taught by William Payne, Ellwood Cubberly, and George Strayer confirmed that educational administration had a knowledge base to solve some of the problems of managing city school districts that consisted primarily of principles of business and accounting, teacher training, and practical advice to their students.

These early professors and students were practical men who needed to find enough teachers, books, and classrooms for burgeoning numbers of public school students (Cooper & Boyd 1987). During the early to mid-1990s, elements of scientific management, social foundations, and the first degrees and licensure in school administration were granted. Within thirty years the knowledge base placed emphasis on required curriculum, the selection and training of greater numbers of qualified teachers, and the necessary skills needed for principals.

While most of the early training of school administrators stressed the managerial control of books, budgets, and buildings, complex social conditions brought about by poverty and prejudice required that school leaders become social architects, hence resulting in greater emphasis on human relations within school leadership preparation (Griffiths 1956). The theory movement was over the next horizon.

The Theory Movement

The 1964 classic *Behavioral Science and Educational Administration*, edited by Dan Griffiths, gave clarion calls to move from practical training of school administrators toward greater emphasis on empirical research, human behavior, and statistical precision driven by administrative theory. In order to gain the same respect in academe given to public administration and business, educational administration professors moved to "change its spots" toward more theoretical and sophisticated modes of inquiry.

The 1954 meeting of the National Council of Professors of Educational Administration (NCPEA) was, by all reports, a cauldron of debate and critical analyses. Several social scientists joined professors of educational administration and challenged the old knowledge base and applied research strategies in the field of school administration.

Thus, by the late 1960s the integration of the social and behavioral sciences led to an emphasis on administrative theory and research to strengthen the knowledge base (Campbell & Gregg 1957; Griffiths 1964; Culberson 1988). One constant through these shifting winds was the search for more respect as a professional discipline in higher education. As a result, the need for stronger theory-based "scientific research" led scholars and critics to create measurable preparation standards and skills that all future school leaders must possess.

But inconsistencies in leadership preparation remained. Culbertson (1983) suggested that the theory movement failed to live up to its advanced billing. He noted that even though theory-based research was promising to add prestige to the field of inquiry, it had not sufficiently addressed the ambiguity around the applications of theory to school practices.

Peterson and Finn (1985) added that perhaps leadership education programs are excessively rigid in content and too loose in application to real school issues. They asked, "Is there a valid relationship between what individuals do in universities in order to become licensed as educational administrators and the actual knowledge, skills, and competencies they need to be effective managers and systems leaders in the public schools?" (48).

However, the theory-practice dilemma led to a very significant epistemological question: "What knowledge is of most value for the field of educational administration?" (Peterson and Finn 1985, 17). While this question demanded answers, there was little doubt that the theory movement and its cloak of academic respectability was here to stay. This search for the holy grail of honor as a discipline led to the creation of what Cooper and Boyd (1987) labeled the "One Best Model." This model is powered by state licensure requirements and examinations, similar courses in facilities, law, personnel, instructional management, and finance, and limited content in the social and behavioral science methods and leadership.

In addition, the university rewards structure requires faculty to seek credibility and promotion with publications in a number of acceptable refereed and high impact journals and textbooks. Griffiths and other pioneers in the theory movement believed that "the road to generalized knowledge can lie only in the tough minded empirical research, not introspection and subjective experience" (Hoy & Miskel 1991, 25). However, others challenged this empirical arrogance as the only way to find respect as a discipline.

Other Voices

The dominant theory movement and the rational One Best Model attracted critics who believed that organizations and people are far too unpredictable to apply rigid, strict mathematical rules and scientific principles to them. Perhaps the most contentious debate occurred between an advocate of the One Best Model and a pioneer advocating the naturalistic postmodern approach.

The "great debates" of the 1970s involved Griffiths, a strong leader advocating a rational theoretical approach, and Thomas Greenfield who stood his ground for the postmodern epistemological view (Greenfield 1975). Greenfield claimed organizations could not be understood under a physical science framing but rather should be investigated using a naturalistic process of observing and recording human behaviors as they occur. He wrote, "Organizations exist only in the minds of people. One cannot touch an organization" (71).

Griffiths (1964) countered Greenfield's position that the scientific approach to leadership preparation is guided by system theory that guides the researcher in describing, predicting, and explaining human behavior within the organization. System theory provides a systematic process to assess program effectiveness as opposed to relying on isolated observations of individuals in the organization. More recent proponents of rationalistic theory include Wayne Hoy and Cecil Miskel (2008) who assert that "[t]heory in educational administration has the same role as theory in physics, chemistry, biology, or psychology—that is, it provides general explanations and guides research" (2).

Greenfield's influence continues to lead others in the belief that the rationalistic methodologies are inadequate to understand the complexities of human interaction and should not be given blind acceptance (Foster 1986; Lincoln & Guba 1985; Murphy & Hallinger 1987; Owens 1995; English 2006; Irby, Brown, & Yang 2009). The battle lines drawn in the late 1970s are less clear today because ongoing dialogue among the two camps has influenced greater numbers of scholars to respect each other and accept the value of both the rationalistic and naturalistic paradigms to add new insights into the growing, changing knowledge base.

Cooper and Boyd (1987) were perhaps the most important voices that challenged scholars to look beyond the rationalistic One Best Model to naturalistic and ethnographic approaches to improve the profession and the preparation of school leaders for the next century. They wrote:

> The training of school administrators must look to modify the system, to making training more rigorous, more interesting, more enticing, and integrated into the real school problems . . . besides reaction against over reliance on the scientific, behavioral model for research and action, interest in increasing in the "naturalistic" studies, those that actually bring the researcher and objects (or "subjects") of study eye to eye. Thus, the ethnographic approaches, case studies, and program evaluations have lifted the student in school administration out of the arm chair and into the school environment (269).

These modifications have proven to be difficult in times of deep divisions among scholars about what is most valued in the scholarship and preparation of future school leaders. The authors take the position that a graduate degree in leadership education without a rigorous course in organizational or leadership theory is like a ship without a rudder. Organizational and leadership theories are the cradle of the discipline and should be emphasized in every program.

Applied Science or Skilled Craft?

As indicated previously, some believe educational leadership is an applied science with a knowledge base (Hoyle 1991; Hoy & Miskel 2008; Lunenburg & Ornstein 2003), requiring empirical research to extend the parameters of scientific knowledge. Others call educational administration a skilled craft (Cicchelli, Marcus, & Weiner 2002), suggesting that to become effective one must learn at the side of a master leader promoting an apprentice-model of leadership preparation. Michael Dantley (2003) and Paul Houston and Steven Sokolow (2006) believe the best approach is helping prospective school leaders develop greater interpersonal and spiritual strength necessary to resist school system inequities and oppression.

Fenwick English (2006) argues that there is not a single field/discipline of educational administration but an amorphous blend of many related lines of inquiry. To limit any of these lines would be deleterious to the profound knowledge of schools and the type of leaders required in an age of constant change. Also, English cautions leadership education about the blind obedience to the American Association of School Administrators

(AASA), Interstate School Leaders Licensure Consortium (ISLLC), and National Council for Accreditation of Teacher Education (NCATE) standards for licensure and preparation. He and other critics of the standards movement claim that the standards are minimum pedestrian benchmarks that have little bearing on how well a principal or superintendent actually leads schools to successful performance.

According to English, the ISLLC standards and the National Policy Board for Educational Administration is the subagency by which "the skill sets and indicators used in practice are supposed to be taught, not only as the be-all and end-all of preparation but when applied to accredit a university-based program, similarly imposes a reduction in its curriculum" (467). This sounds very similar to the concerns Cooper and Boyd (1987) had about the One Best Model twenty years previously after the introduction of the *AASA Guidelines for the Preparation of School Administrators* (Hoyle 1983).

The caution about the misuse of preparation standards was issued by Hoyle, English, and Steffy (1985) with the following statement:

> AASA recognizes the danger inherent in developing *Guidelines* that may vary substantially from the programs provided by some institutions. Professionalism depends on creativity and the capacity of individuals and institutions to capitalize on these unique strengths. Since uniform standards rigidly applied may impair the flexibility that programs need to meet local and regional needs, AASA desires that these *Guidelines* not be used to limit program development or the expertise of a given faculty (4).

Thus, the modern standards movement, perhaps unintentionally, strengthened the rational, scientific, and controlling world of the One Best Model with the creation of the AASA *Guidelines*. These guidelines created the initial basic competences and skills added to university programs and became the basic "footprints" found in the ISLLC/NCATE *Standards for Advanced Programs in Educational Leadership* (2008).

Few leadership education programs can ignore teaching these standards that represent entry-level knowledge, skills, and functions of the discipline and require a passing score on the licensure examination. In addition, most leadership preparation programs are accredited by NCATE, which centers on the ISLLC standards. However, heated debate continues about the value of minimum standards that critics find too narrow and appear to exclude broader preparation in social/cultural, political, and financial complexities surrounding schools and schooling that enervate the best school leaders.

Trying to bring consensus among professors about the value of standards in improving leadership education is a major challenge. However, the standards are embedded in the curriculum of most graduate programs and the number of programs grows each year to meet the future need for principals and superintendents.

Programs Proliferate

Despite the growing need to prepare greater numbers of school administrators, observers are concerned about the perceived standardization of both traditional and online programs that may be diminishing the quality among the 371 programs taught by over 3,000 professors preparing principals and superintendents (Creighton, Lunenburg, Irby, & Nie 2004). With a greater number of degree outlets, rigor and quality have become more suspect.

Today 57 percent or 211 of the 371 graduate programs offer the doctorate and 116 of the programs offer only the Ed.D. Forty-four programs offer only the Ph.D., and fifty-nine offer both the Ed.D. and Ph.D. Since the early 1980s, the Ed.D. accounts for most of the increase in new programs and much of the criticism. The rapid expansion of new Ed.D. programs has caused ire among critics who claim that many of the new programs lack academic rigor and include excessive numbers of core classes taught by adjunct professors with minimum academic qualifications.

Some critics contend that the growing number of online administration degrees and licensure programs emphasize credit counting rather than crucial practical and theoretical knowledge and skill acquisition. While this critical picture may not be accurate, little research exists in the area of leadership education programming quality to refute such claims.

Moreover, markers of quality in leadership education programs differ widely and no consensus exists at this time (Torres & Hoyle, 2008). Regardless of these growing quality concerns, the pace to accelerate the selection and preparation of more principals and superintendents will persist unabated. The projected mass retirement of principals and superintendents is alarming, and professors of educational administration have no choice but to face the facts, recruit more talented, caring young leaders, and revamp preparation programs to meet the needs of more diverse student populations.

Commission Reports

Numerous commissions have produced reports calling for reform in leadership education and the removal of weaker programs. These reports question the value of university leadership education and their lack of success in preparing qualified, aspiring principals and system administrators. Perhaps the most influential leadership education reform report was produced by the National Commission on Excellence in Educational

Administration (NCEEA; Griffiths, Stout, & Forsyth 1988). The report states, "What the field of educational administration accepts for certification and licensure is recognized more for its weaknesses than by its strengths" (9).

Moreover, this report called for closer collaboration between university preparation programs and public schools, increasing the numbers of minorities and women in the field and strengthening student selection criteria. In addition, the commission was the first to recommend closing "cash cow" programs with inadequate numbers of faculty and inadequate financial support. No programs were shut down, but the recommendation led to the creation of the Educational Leadership Constituent Council (ELCC) that evaluated preparation programs and publicly identified those with outdated curriculum and lack of focus on state and national standards.

ELCC examined licensure and degree programs for their applications of standards to licensure established first by AASA (Hoyle 1983, 1993) and the 1996 ISLLC standards. However, while some programs were admonished by the ELCC, few if any were actually closed.

National Policy Board for Educational Administration (NPBEA), ELCC, and NCATE will continue to monitor the quality and direction of leadership education with the hope that their influence will raise a loud alarm about the need for superior preparation programs and the need for additional funding from the universities and agencies. If the U.S. schools are to help every child find success, then programs in leadership education need greater financial support and respect from governing agencies.

Other Critics of Preparation

According to many critics, administrator preparation programs are too heavy on theory and too light on practice. According to Hale and Moorman (2003), "[t]he course work is poorly sequenced and organized, making it impossible to scaffold the learning . . . and students do not have mentored opportunities to develop practical understanding of real-world job competencies" (9).

The ELCC admonishments of administrator preparation programs were a primary reason some school superintendents in suburban and urban school districts created leadership academies to select and prepare their own future administrators. In addition, nonuniversity agencies such as the Broad Foundation provided support for an urban superintendent preparation program and funding for various research projects.

Christine DeVita, (2007) President of the Wallace Foundation and Broad Foundation underwriter writes, "Study after study has shown that the training principals typically receive in university programs and from their own districts doesn't do nearly enough to prepare them for their roles as leaders of learners" (i).

This overriding concern about principal preparation prompted the Wallace Foundation to fund the recent report *Preparing School Leaders for a Changing World: Lessons from Exemplary Leadership Development Programs* (2007). Authors Linda Darling-Hammond, Michelle LaPointe, Debra Meyerson, Margaret Terry Orr, and Carol Cohen repeated much of what has been claimed for over fifty years calling the knowledge base of principal preparation programs out of date and irrelevant to real-world school operations. They claimed that most programs they examined are underfunded and lack successful internship or clinical experiences for future school leaders and asserted that most professional development for school administrators lacks systematic focus on teaching and student learning.

This report merely reinforces much of what previous observers of leadership education knew about the deficiencies found in numerous, but not all, university principal and system leadership preparation programs. The authors suggest that "recruiting the right people, preparing them comprehensively, and supporting them as they lead schools is essential to improve the pool of available school leaders" (5). This is old wine in expensive well-funded new wine bottles.

Again, this report critical of leadership education by Linda Darling-Hammond and the other writers provides little research evidence or professional advice about improving programs that prepare principals who actually improve student achievement and create higher performing learning communities. Without this piece of the puzzle, the report is a replication of similar "expert" studies with little program outcome data. The information they do provide spreads the alarm but leaves the reader asking for more empirical evidence.

The loudest critic of leadership education in recent years, Art Levine (2005) in his epic report *Educating School Leaders*, soundly denounced school leadership preparation and doctoral programs citing outdated curriculum, weak standards, and poor financial support for faculty, students, and programs. The commission chaired by Levine consisted of agency directors, former university administrators, a former National Endowment for the Arts (NEA) executive, and a college dean. No active professor of educational administration was a member of the writing team.

The report portrays most administrator preparation programs as "inadequate to appalling" with most university administrators unwilling to engage in any measure of "systematic self-assessment" (Levine 2005, 1). He called most of the rapidly growing graduate programs "cash cows" that help university administrators support other graduate programs struggling with low enrollments. Thus, Levine was more emphatic than the previous 1998 NCEEA report by declaring that most, if not all, Ed.D. programs should be replaced by a master's degree similar to the MBA degree.

Levine's stinging report about leadership education programs evoked an outcry from professors of educational administration and particularly his colleagues at Teachers College. Quick to respond were leaders in University Council for Professors of Educational Administration and the NCPEA. Young, Creighton, Crow, Orr, and Ogawa (2005) led the rebuttal by writing, "Across the nation, many scholars, policy makers, policy analysts, school leaders, professional organizations, and foundations have been addressing this need for years" (1).

Achilles (2005) challenged the veracity of the Levine report by writing, "The Levine report is repetitive because of its headlong dash into ideology and its relaxed newsy tone . . . and includes only a cursory view of prior research and scholarship, calling into question its own scholarship and sincerity" (1).

And as in the previous Wallace Foundation funded report about school principals, Levine and his commission claim that leadership education is inadequate and should be drastically changed and many programs eliminated. Although Levine's *Educating School Leaders* (2005) provides little empirical evidence about the success of graduates in actually leading schools and lacks structured interviews with faculty and current students, the negative generalizations overpowered any positive findings that may have emerged from the programs. Levine and his editors claim to have applied the following criteria for judging program quality:

1. Purpose: The program's purpose is explicit, focusing on the education of practicing school leaders.
2. Curriculum coherence: The curriculum mirrors program purposes and goals.
3. Curriculum balance: The curriculum integrates the theory and practice of administration.
4. Faculty composition: The faculty includes academics and practitioners.
5. Admissions: Admissions criteria are designed to recruit students with the capacity and motivation to become school leaders.
6. Degrees: Graduation standards are high.
7. Research: Research carried out in the program is of high quality, driven by practice.
8. Finances: Resources are adequate to support the program.
9. Assessment: The program engaged in continuing self-assessment and improving of its performance.

While these nine criteria are remarkably similar to those promoted in the 1960s, the Levine report serves little guidance as to meeting the nine criteria. With no attempt to recommend databased improvements or methods to assess the success of the programs and their graduates, it is not surprising that some perceive Levine's findings as broad brush indictments.

While Levine is due some credit for stimulating much-needed discussion around leadership preparation, the report itself falls short of fully addressing fundamental aspects. In point of fact, many of the criteria in the Levine report for determining program quality were already established in most master's and doctoral programs in the United States and Canada. Levine and his commission also appeared to overlook critical markers of success and failure such as how graduates fared in their present leadership roles.

However, we agree that some programs overly rely on adjunct professors with limited expertise or hire faculty having little or no experience in school administration. In recent years, leadership education programs with both large and small numbers of faculty suffer gross imbalances between clinical and research-oriented faculty. According to McCarthy and Kuh (1997), only 30 percent of faculty members at comprehensive regional universities have prior experience in school administration or have been closely connected to professional administrator associations. These institutions prepare the majority of school administrators across the country.

In contrast to the regional doctoral programs, McCarthy and Kuh (1997) found that only 8 percent of the faculty at research-one universities had prior experience in public school administration. Fifteen years later, Levine also found a small percentage of the faculty at research-one university leadership education programs had limited or no public or private school administrative experience. To be sure, the primary impetus for certain research-one university programs is preparing students for faculty positions or careers in public policy.

For instance, in 2006, seven of the full-time doctoral students at Stanford University in educational policy and administration reported preparing for careers in university research or policy and none were considering careers as principals and superintendents at the time (Hoyle & Torres, 2006). Similar programs (e.g., the University of Michigan, the University of Texas at Austin, the Pennsylvania State University, and Indiana University) were also found to be preparing students for higher education or governmental policy roles but to a far more limited extent.

In recent years, tier-one leadership education programs have experienced a drop in the number of students seeking the master's degree and principal certification resulting in the majority of these students enrolling in regional universities. Whether all these aspects together signal an alarming trend is a question beyond the scope of this book. Yet, few would argue that a balance of real-world experience and highly relevant scholarship is what all preparation programs should strive for.

LEADERSHIP PREPARATION AND SUCCESSFUL PRACTICES

Perhaps the growing number of leadership education faculty with no administrative experience is one reason for the limited research-seeking relationships between what is taught in graduate leadership education programs and successful practices of school administrators. It is not surprising that many new faculty have few contacts in the field since they rarely attend national, state, or regional principal or superintendent conferences.

This isolation is a primary reason that many school administrators feel that coursework is too theoretical and bears little relevance to practice. Some research-one university professors claim the "best and brightest" candidates find practitioner-oriented programs less appealing due to a lack of intellectual rigor and desire their degree from a more "prestigious" institution. These perceptions, real or not, must be changed if leadership education research is to close the gap between preparation and student achievement.

Other potential school leaders observe the growing public pressures of student accountability, school finances, and board politics and choose other career paths. Regardless of the reasons, superintendents are concerned about the diminishing talent pool among prospective principals, and superintendent search firms find their lists of qualified candidates dwindling each year.

These issues lead some observers to believe that leadership education programs attract students with less promise who enter through self-selection. Still others believe that the number of talented future school leaders is improving each year and that preparation programs are more intellectually challenging and relevant to practice than critics suggest. (Hoyle 2005, 2007a; Murphy 2006; Orr 2006)

Since the early 1990s, numerous research studies reveal limited but credible "hard descriptive findings" about how students find that the skills and knowledge taught in their graduate programs actually improved their practice. However, the findings fall short in measuring the extent to which the skills and dispositions taught in graduate leadership programs actually improve their practices. This measurement problem is confounded by the diversity of leadership preparation programs across the county.

A report by the Wallace Foundation, *Becoming a leader: Preparing principals for today's schools* (2008), recommends that state departments of education bring uniformity to leadership preparation by improving the design and quality of principal preparation through tougher entry standards, more rigorous standards-based curriculum, and relevant internship requirements. However, neither state department administrators nor Wallace foundation writers realize the shortfalls in creating one best model for improving principal and superintendent training.

The authors of the Wallace report agree that for the range of challenges leaders confront in the nation's estimated 106,000 public elementary and secondary schools, there is no magic formula for dramatically improving principal training (Wallace Foundation Report 2008). The report gleans four broad lessons in increasing the quality of leadership preparation in the nation. They are as follows:

> Lesson One: Successful principal training programs are significantly different from the majority of programs in existence. They are more selective, more focused on improvement of instruction, more closely tied to the needs of districts, and provide more relevant internships with hands-on leadership experiences.
>
> Lesson Two: Leadership training should not end when principals are hired. It should continue with high quality mentoring for new principals and with professional development for all principals to promote career-long growth in line with the evolving needs of schools and districts.
>
> Lesson Three: High quality leader development can make a real difference, but providing it can involve added costs. Resources therefore should be directed at quality programs with proven benefits.
>
> Lesson Four: Fixing what is wrong with leadership preparation is essential, but not enough. Addressing the leadership challenge also requires remedying the difficult working conditions that can undermine even the best-trained principals (5–9).

While these four lessons are hardly new in the literature, they need to be stressed to all parties engaged in school leadership improvement. A casual look at textbooks and particularly the annual NCPEA yearbook reinforces the same four lessons presented in the 2008 Wallace Foundation Report. Champions for improved administrator preparation continue stressing these lessons and many more in their teaching, research, and writing. As a result, signs of progress have emerged about administrator leadership in school improvement, especially practices that improve student performance on a variety of measures (Hoyle 2005, 2007b; Murphy & Vriesenga 2005).

Since the early years of leadership education programs, observers have sought to improve the selection of graduate students, make the curriculum more challenging and relevant to improving schools, and focus greater attention on course work and projects requiring skills in student assessment and data analysis. These vital skills assist the new school leader in applying data to improving the performance of all students. Moreover, financial support is meager to enrich internship experiences that are closely linked with class content and emphasize the role of school leader who understands and promotes the technical core of teaching and learning.

At the center of the technical core of schooling is student achievement data. Many successful school administrators know how to help create a culture of success and assist teachers in closing achievement gaps that help each student on a daily basis. Well-prepared school leaders have improved skills in using data to monitor student achievement to improve instruction by (a) distributing leadership throughout each classroom and campus to nurture communities of learners, (b) distributing disaggregated data about student achievement to staff and all stakeholders, (c) viewing student learning as a system wide responsibility, and most importantly, (d) using disaggregated student achievement data to make decisions about resource reallocation to enhance student learning—the main thing (Shidemantle & Hoyle 2004; Hoyle 2007a; Hoyle, Bjork, Collier, & Glass 2005, 155–156).

As a field, professors experience dissonance about best ways to prepare educational leaders and the directions of empirical research needed to inform best practices in administrator preparation. Consequently, this debate fuels criticisms by both insiders and outsiders to the leadership preparation enterprise.

This lack of a clear understanding about what leadership preparation programs should be and what content, instructional methods, and structures should frame them is at the heart of the tensions. There is growing debate about what to call these leadership preparation programs, with names ranging from educational leadership to administration and supervision, policy, or instructional leadership.

Where are the excellent programs? A recent comprehensive study of top-ranked leadership education doctoral programs conducted by Hoyle and Torres (2008) found positive responses from successful graduates. The researchers found that doctoral graduates of six of the top ranked programs (i.e., Harvard, Ohio State, Penn State, Stanford, Teachers College Columbia, and Wisconsin-Madison) gave effusive praise to their programs and faculty.

Graduates of the six programs, who are now serving as administrators in high-performing public and private schools, were eager to praise their doctoral programs' relevance to their successful practices. However, all were concerned that several of their "big picture" professors had retired and programs were drifting away from the more structured coursework and internships relevant to the real world of schools.

Realizing the complexities of leading schools, several graduates and current students lamented professors giving minimal attention to NCATE standards and the traditional knowledge base of educational administration. Despite concerns about the relevance of the knowledge base, graduates and current students in six of the top ranked institutions gave positive responses about their doctoral programs.

The notion that educational leadership preparation programs are lacking in quality has gained momentum in recent years, becoming ingrained in our collective belief system. However, Hoyle's (2007b) response to this line of self-abuse is "bunk. . . . Our [research] subjects regardless of which university they graduated from or what kind of school they are now serving in, praised their preparation" (3).

While one may intuitively predict graduates of top ranked programs to be proud of their degrees, the research clearly indicated that the former students believe that these doctoral programs are preparing leaders for schools. Feedback from leadership program graduates is nothing new. However, the reviews rarely gather data on how successful the graduate is in leading schools that actually improve student achievement and learning communities over a three- to four-year time period.

Based on this study of top-ranked programs, we recommend that program planners adapt their eight interview questions found in Step Six to conduct their own quality reviews. Previous studies reveal positive feedback from graduates of both master's and doctoral programs (Jackson & Kelly 2002; Hoyle 2005). Based on these limited program review efforts, we believe that most leadership education program graduates will also provide surprisingly positive feedback on the value of their graduate experiences on their leadership capabilities.

While a limited number of studies reveal promising results, more stringent research methods and real-time data are needed to determine more accurate measures of program quality and the success of graduates in leading schools and districts to higher performance. Educational administration is not the only field that struggles with outcome data about the success of their graduates. The next section is an overview of difficulty in related management/leadership disciplines in finding better links between academic preparation and graduates' job performance.

LEADERSHIP PREPARATION AND SUCCESSFUL PRACTICE IN RELATED FIELDS

Educational administration is not the only professional discipline that suffers a gap between what is taught and the practical applications. Relationships between graduate program course content and successful business practices continue to puzzle researchers in business management. Jeenie Woo (1986) found that advanced degrees in industry have salary advantages, but the degree has negligible influence on job performance, measures of salary growth, performance ratings, or promotion.

According to Nathan and Cascio (1986), the greatest flaw in management assessment in education and industry is the weak link to the job itself. The research literature on industrial and organizational psychology investigating university preparation and job performance is sparse. It is also surprising that research of on-the-job training rarely reports measurable relationships between the training and job performance.

The literature does report that education and training are vital to ensure that all employees are engaged in their work. Other studies report that training employees helps them to develop a positive orientation toward their work and their organization and helps ensure that employees understand and believe in the vision of the company (Singam 2007). Winfred Arthur (2007), a Texas A&M University scholar of organizational psychology, concurs with the 22-year-old findings by Nathan and Cascio and other researchers that few statistical relationships exist between formal university training and success in the business and manufacturing world.

Thus, based on these missing links between preparation and job performance in business and industry, it is not surprising to us that research findings are scarce between leadership education and work performance of principals and superintendents.

ASSESSMENT CENTERS

One attempt to solve the preparation/production dilemma is the use of assessment centers to provide for the assessment and selection of management personnel (Arthur & Benjamin 1999). According to Thornton (1992), assessment centers have made some progress in evaluating personnel performance in a more valid, reliable, and systematic way. Assessors claim to produce more accurate predictions of managerial success than traditional paper-and-pencil tests and personality profile measures.

Thornton defines an assessment center as "[a] comprehensive, standardized procedure in which multiple assessment techniques such as situation exercises and simulations are used to evaluate individual employees for various purposes." In these centers, numerous techniques are used (e.g., situation exercises, leaderless discussions, business games, and presentations) to assess participants on behavioral dimensions or competencies such as team building, decision making, organizing, budgeting, and planning (Hoyle et al. 2005). However, assessment centers are not the complex real world of either business or education, and little research is available to support their value in selecting successful leaders.

In the early 1980s, the National Association of Secondary School Principals (NASSP) created as assessment center that evaluated participants on twelve skill dimensions. Research on the NASSP assessment effort revealed that assessment centers help identify promising candidates for the position of principal because the overall ratings received are valid, reliable, and related to the real day-to-day job of a principal. The centers, however, proved to be expensive and very labor-intensive to operate. The cost per individual ranged from $500 to $1,500 and the skills established for benchmark performance had not been consistently tested.

A less expensive modified form of the NASSP model is being used as part of the selection criteria in some school districts and university leadership programs. The less costly and time-consuming version of the NASSP Assessment Center Model is the *Web-based NASSP Leadership Skills Assessment Program* (2008). Four tools are included in the model: Analysis of Development Assets and Needs Assessment, a 360-degree Self- and Observer Assessment, an In-Basket Performance Assessment, and a Development Planning Activity and Guide for Reflection and Decision Making.

The software enables users to produce a list of suggestions for professional development. The suggestions are based on a "final report" that compiles data from the assessment tools. The program's tools are built on the findings and practices from over twenty years of work in skills assessment in education with business and industry. The skills examined correlate highly with the *Educational Leadership Policy Standards: ISLLC 2008.*

Studies reveal mixed results as to the effectiveness of assessment centers compared to more conventional methods. However, there is some evidence that the model is a valid tool for determining the presence of strengths and improvement needs. The NASSP and other assessment center models fall short in predicting success on the job but agree about important predictors of leadership success of an employee in previous leadership positions (i.e., a pattern of servant leadership and persuasive skills to inspire and inform members of the organization; Hoyle 2002).

PROMISING SIGNS FOR LEADERSHIP EDUCATION

More recently, a promising body of research has increased the knowledge base around preparation and professional development of school principals. Ken Leithwood (2007), Tim Waters (2007), and a taskforce in the *SLPPS* (2009) project are a few who have been drawn to the conundrum between what leaders are taught and how well they actually lead. Perhaps the most comprehensive list of references on the topic is included in the research references compiled by the expert panel appointed by the

NPBEA to revise the ISLLC standards. The expert panel focused on the research base for updating the standards and attaching a rich plethora of research literature for the updated standards (www.csso.net).

The rich body of research and best practice references, however, remains limited about the predictive reliability between preparation and practice that should be incorporated into our programs in order to prepare exemplary school leaders. However limited the predictive data, professors must take the findings and advance the field through ongoing inquiry. Charles Achilles (2009) believes all scholars must focus on school improvement studies and use an evolving knowledge base to find the missing links between administrative behaviors and student performance. Achilles has "little patience with professors, practitioners, and policy persons who do not understand, keep up with, or do robust research, theory development, and exemplary practice" (72).

Many professors and practicing school administrators are positive in their assessment of the state of leadership education. They believe that university preparation of school principals and superintendents has never been better. This positive perception of improvement in leadership education prevails at the annual meeting of the NCPEA. Members of NCPEA serve a wide range of regional universities who prepare the majority of school administrators for schools in the United States.

Members of NCPEA and faculty in University Council for Educational Administration (UCEA) departments claim their programs have improved their student admissions criteria, increased the ethnic and gender diversity of the students and faculty, found more financial support from central administration, and are conducting more research seeking evidence about the impact of preparation on successful practice (McCarthy 1999; Glass, Bjork, & Brunner 2000; Jackson & Kelley 2002; Achilles 2005; Hoyle 2005; Murphy 2006; Orr 2006; Hoyle & Torres 2008).

Terry Orr (2006) contends that despite limited evidence that leadership preparation directly improves student learning at the campus and district levels, some of the criticism is earned and some not. She records notable successes in leadership education across the country and that "leadership education programs are striving for a deeper understanding of the role of leadership, but also as a means of promoting social justice and democracy" (489). In addition, Jerome Murphy (2006) and many professors of educational administration believe that a number of leadership preparation programs are much better than critics suggest.

Thus, the main thesis of this book is that if leadership education programs are to become relevant and respected by both academia and the world of practice, we must repeat what Cooper and Boyd (1987) and many others have confirmed: all leadership education programs must stress the following:

1. a driving purpose; create the most relevant and rigorous curriculum and instructional delivery;
2. integrate theory with successful best practices;
3. seek a balance in faculty between full-time scholars and clinical practitioners;
4. admit the best and brightest—more importantly—the most committed servant leaders;
5. conduct high quality research and writing focused on school improvement;
6. seek adequate resources from the central administration and other sources to provide support to faculty, staff and students; and
7. conduct ongoing assessment of leadership effectiveness of graduates serving as school administrators.

We believe that the majority of all graduate programs in leadership education have caring and talented faculty, capable students with a personal mission to serve students, curriculum linked to national standards, and also intellectual challenges to produce reflective practicing school leaders.

While critics will continue to seek flaws in leadership education either real or imagined, we believe criticism motivates us to work even harder to implement what we know about leadership preparation and give total commitment to preparing the best possible leaders for every child in schools in the United States. The combined years of our experience in education exceeds sixty years. Perhaps our experiences as teachers, administrators, and scholars are of some value to the reader struggling, as we are, to prepare the best possible school leaders for all children and youth.

Questions Remain

The ferment regarding the best research methods, standards and models, and program quality has not answered the big question and the thrust of this book: How do we prepare exemplary school superintendents and principals for schools in the United States? While this book is not the final word, we aspire to create the best guide in the field.

We are very aware that critics of leadership education programs challenge minimum student selection criteria for entry into the degree and certification programs; they question the quality of professors' ability to teach the course content and also prepare students to practice and succeed on the job. Criticism continues about the selection of candidates, relevance of what is taught, how it is taught, and the silent or fragile research links between what is taught and its impact on graduates becoming successful school leaders.

ONE RESPONSE TO CRITICISM: ALTERNATIVE DELIVERY MODELS

The criticism and limited research about the impact of many traditional educational leadership programs and the competition for students has perhaps promoted an increase in alternative delivery modes. The competition for student enrollments is a primary reason for the growing number of online degree and alternative certification programs each academic year. This rapid uncontrolled growth in cyber leadership preparation has prompted program planners to question the quality and integrity of online degree and licensure programs.

The numbers of graduate students in educational leadership enrolling in online licensure and degree programs is especially troubling for traditionalists in the field. Some of the more prominent nontraditional, online programs created by the University of Phoenix, Nova University, Western Governors University, and others enroll thousands of aspiring school leaders each semester. While the course content of these and other online degree programs is similar to those offered in traditional programs, traditionalists are dubious about the extent and quality of authentic interactions among students and with the professor, as well as the integrity in assessing student knowledge and administrative performance.

Lamar University in Texas initiated the *Lamar University Academic Partnership*, an online master's degree in educational leadership. At a cost of $4,950, students are able to complete the program in 18 months. The course content is similar to traditional programs and all requirements can be fulfilled without students having to visit the Lamar University campus. Over 2,000 students were enrolled in the program in June 2009.

Thus far, there has been no evidence reported about the quality of the program or the passing rate of prospective principals on the state licensure examination. However, observers are very dubious about the small number of professors teaching in the program attempting to advise large numbers of online students. What are the quality benchmarks for these online programs? Some use electronic portfolios that include research papers and internship activities. With so few faculty overseeing students' work, the issue of quality becomes the elephant in the room.

Chat rooms and online dialogue between professors and students are viewed by critics as inferior to face-to-face meetings and student cohorts sharing their successes, failures, and mealtimes with professors. Graduates of online programs may be successful in passing the ISLLC licensure examination, but some question if they will be prepared to work in team settings and grasp the dynamics of school politics and organizations. These questions remain unanswered without solid research conducted about the impact of online versus face-to-face leadership education programs.

The time and effort taken to create online classes can prove to be very helpful in emphasizing the most relevant content and projects for a successful learning experience. Online degrees and licensure deserve greater attention by scholars in our field to be sure. The delicate balance between online, hybrid, and face-to-face teaching and mentoring must be carefully monitored to assure that our graduates are capable of leading teachers, patrons, and students to higher performance as productive and caring citizens.

In a recent study of online master's degree students in Educational Leadership at the University of Colorado, researchers found that online degrees were driven to some extent by lucrative financial rewards, market share, and service to students. Yet concerns abound about the quality of such programs. This concern is especially true when it comes to preparing individuals for work in the professions (Ramirez, Burnett, Meagher, Garcia & Lewis 2009, 68).

CAN SCHOOL LEADERS BE PREPARED ELECTRONICALLY?

Several regional universities in Pennsylvania offer online master's degrees and principal certification that has created a challenge to the more traditional programs. Since the creation of the online degrees, the traditional on-campus programs are struggling to attract aspiring principals willing to attend classes in the summer, evenings, and/or weekends. There is little research evidence to guide program planners about the best balance between cyber and face-to-face leadership education programs.

The unanswered question is "can we adequately prepare school leaders by wire?" Research is needed to investigate the missing links between these cyber preparation programs and their long-range impact on educating school administrators who can actually lead schools to high performance and build successful learning communities.

As the faculty at Lamar University have discovered, perhaps the greatest threat to quality is capacity. That is, how many students can be adequately mentored in cyber versus face-to-face educational leadership programs? It is vital to find this delicate balance between cyber and face-to-face mentoring and teaching methods in both the master's and doctoral degree programs. Passing exit examinations is only one measure of program quality, and the jury is out on the effectiveness of cyber graduates in leading effective schools.

Many faculty members from traditional programs are expressing concern that students seek online programs mainly because of easy access and less demanding degree requirements and certification. As one might conclude, it is very difficult to assist online cyber students in finding administrator positions when they rarely engage in face-to-face conversations with principals, superintendents, or personnel directors. We extend this discussion in the following section.

The Slippery Rock Model

In response to competition from cyber programming, Slippery Rock University of Pennsylvania has created a master's degree for school leaders that includes a rich balance of face-to-face on campus classes, hybrid classes (i.e., one-half online, the other half on campus) and a few classes offered online. The new program is grounded in the standards-based curriculum, research methods, and foundations and supported by an influential advisory team consisting of area school leaders (i.e., superintendents and principals).

Members of the advisory team are frequently invited to campus for meetings and dinners and to help teach classes, serve as mentors to aspiring administrators, and provide internship experiences that may involve research and evaluation projects needed by each district. Each new cohort class begins in the summer with a three-day academy for all master's degree students in administration, curriculum, and special education. This three-day academy includes speakers and projects that emphasize building learning communities among the students from the three program areas.

In addition, this rich three-day experience includes barbecues to increase interaction time and encourages students in curriculum and special education to seek certification as principals. Also, the administration students are introduced to the content and value of course work in curriculum and instruction and how to collaborate in creating programs for students having special needs. The Slippery Rock model is attractive to prospective students because of the personal attention and mentoring by the faculty and strong collaboration among university faculty and administration and school leaders.

Each student will be assigned a public school administrator who will mentor them throughout the course work. The students are very aware the Slippery Rock program can lead to possible administrative positions in area school districts. These connections are less likely to occur in online degree and certification programs if no effort is made to establish personal relationships.

EXEMPLARY LEADERSHIP PREPARATION PROGRAMS

Imitation of quality leadership education programs is a form of flattery. There is no need to rediscover what other programs have found to be successful in preparing leaders who have improved schools and school districts. It is important to investigate the strengths and needs of both top ranked and lower ranked programs. Some highly ranked doctoral programs focus less on preparation and more on producing policy analysts. Other highly ranked programs strive to maintain a balance between scholarly productivity and preparing school principals and superintendents.

As indicated previously, in the past twenty years, the lower ranked regional university programs have produced the majority of the principals and superintendents in the United States and perhaps claim to offer more practical models for preparing school leaders. Thus, quality among professors and programs in educational administration varies, but the best preparation programs must not be overlooked due to popular ranking systems. Research and practical observations of a wide variety of graduate programs bring us to believe that caution should be taken when judging quality based on outdated or irrelevant ranking criteria. After reviewing numerous master's and doctoral degree plans, we provide four model plans (see appendix B).

ASSUMPTIONS

It is with this backdrop that we offer six steps to preparing exemplary principals and superintendents. However, these six steps are grounded in the assumption that the following conditions should be met in order to support the six steps for preparing exemplary school leaders.

Assumption One: Human capacity is available to support the goals of the programs. The master's degree/certification program includes at least two full-time tenure track professors advising and teaching the students. The doctoral program includes at least three full-time tenure track professors and three part-time adjunct/clinical professors with current or prior public or private school administrative experience. These full-time faculty and part-time faculty teach, serve on master's and doctoral committees, and attend faculty meetings concerning student admissions, advisement, curriculum, instruction, student examinations, internships, and dissertation quality. This total commitment by all faculty members is vital to successful leadership education for all students.

Assumption Two: Programs are driven by benchmarks of quality and rigor. The master's and doctoral programs in educational administration meet NCATE, regional, and state accreditation requirements. This is primarily aimed at university programs offering master's degrees and licensure of future school administrators.

Assumption Three: Programs continuously monitor efficiency and effectiveness. Student numbers are limited to forty in the master's degree principal program (with two full-time faculty) and no more than forty-five part-time doctoral students (with three full-time faculty). For every additional fifteen part-time doctoral students add one full-time tenure track professor and one active adjunct/clinical faculty member.

Assumption Four: Fiscal resources are available to carry out the goals of the programs. The financial support from the college or school and central administration is adequate for staff support and faculty travel for internship supervision and travel to state and at least one national conference. In addition, every master's and doctoral degree program has an external advisory body consisting of school superintendents, principals, and region service center directors that meets three times a year.

This body serves two major functions: to advise faculty on the relevance of course content to actual practice and to assist faculty in placing students in internship real-world learning serving as adjunct professors for the program when needed. In addition, it is assumed the faculty is adequately supported with reliable technologies and technicians for online and traditional teaching.

Assumption Five: Students of high quality are selected. Students are selected for both the master's and doctoral programs based on the following criteria.

1. Candidates have a proven record of servant leadership in teaching, community service, and other activities. We believe that this attribute is the most important criterion in selecting potential school leaders. If the applicant has been a selfless leader in past roles as a youth in scouting, school, university, and in his or her community, this leadership pattern usually continues. If the applicant has little or no record of serving others and has little penchant for assuming leadership positions, he or she should be advised to look for another graduate area. Also, student applications include letters of recommendation from former and current professors, supervisors, peers, civic, religious, and employees in organizations where the candidate held leadership positions.
2. The candidate has a combined score of least 1,000 on the math and language areas of the graduate record examination (GRE). A few exceptions to these scores may be made based on strong evidence of the candidate's work record, but best practice reveals that doctoral students with scores ranging from (950 to 1,200 perform better than doctoral students with scores ranging from 780 to 850. This is

applicable when it comes to advising students who are conducting research and writing papers and dissertations.

3. The candidate has acceptable writing skills based on the assessment by three faculty members. While good writing is expected for the potential master's student, expectations are higher for the doctoral candidate. The writing should be done while the prospective student is on campus for the interview.
4. The candidate will be interviewed for admission to both the master's and doctoral programs. If travel distance prohibits the face-to-face interview, then satellite television or speaker telephone can be used. The interview questions include inquiries into prior servant leadership activities and about the candidate's vision of inclusive high-performing schools and his or her role in making the visions happen.

Assumption Six: Students are individualized and a growth plan is established. Upon admittance, the master's students will take a Leadership Skills Inventory (LSI) to gather information about students' skill levels from the 2008 *ISLLC Educational Leadership Policy Standards*. Entry-level master's degree students should not be intimidated by their lack of knowledge and actual participation in the thirty-one LSI skills and functions. The LSI is a way to provide faculty with the experience and knowledge levels of beginning aspiring principals.

The latest version of the *Educational Leadership Policy Standards* includes most of the skills and dispositions found in previous versions offered by ELCC, AASA, and NCATE or state standards. Extensive suggested readings are available to support the six standards and related functions can be downloaded at www.ccsso.org or contact Council of Chief State School Officers, One Massachusetts Avenue, NW, Suite 700, Washington, D.C. 20001-1431.

Doctoral students will complete a pre-test requiring essay responses about practical applications of the following areas of scholarship: organizational theories, education law, economic effectiveness and efficiency, social/demographic issues impacting school dropout data in urban and rural areas, and systems modeling and quality school outcome measures, including student performance among diverse cultures and populations.

Three or four faculty plus an adjunct faculty member will evaluate the responses and then discuss the results with each student. Based on the results, student degree programs and course requirements will reflect as much individually prescribed instruction as possible, while maintaining a sequential course pattern for all students. This extra step for content mastery is an extra load on the professor, but we recommend it in order to help beginning students fill in gaps in their knowledge base before enrolling in their first doctoral-level class.

Assumption Seven: Student support through committees is enduring, real-world based, and nurturing. Each master's degree advisory committee consists of two tenured faculty and one adjunct or clinical professor. The adjunct professor who is currently or has recently served as a school administrator is important in creating and monitoring a meaningful internship experience for the student. The doctoral advisory committee consists of three tenured faculty plus one clinical faculty member. Two of the tenured and the clinical members should be in educational administration while the third should be in a related discipline within or out of the college.

The committee chair is the primary advisor for the students and schedules all exams and is in close communication with other committee members on the student's doctoral committee. Finally, the concern about dissertation quality is found in all doctoral programs. We assume that faculty will conduct semiannual departmental seminars to assist in improving skills in both quantitative and qualitative research methods.

While this approach may be out of the ordinary for some faculty, it is a proven strategy in improving the quality of dissertations. Quality dissertations will lead to presentations at national conferences and coauthored publications in respected journals and books. This should help increase the academic reputation of the program. (See appendix A for Criteria to Assess Dissertation Quality.)

Assumption Eight: Auxiliary support is present to support program ends. An effective administrative assistant/director of academic advising should be in place to oversee student admissions, graduate financial aid and assistantships, degree programming, and graduate school policies. The success of many quality graduate programs in educational leadership depends upon this important first contact person who coordinates many of the administrative details for faculty and students. This person is vital to program communications to faculty, students, and to the offices of the dean and university.

Assumption Nine: The student masters all relevant aspects of the leadership curriculum. All course content for the master's degree plans should align with the 2008 *Educational Leadership Policy Standards* or state standards. Faculty members are encouraged to distribute his or her course syllabi to all colleagues to avoid extreme overlap in course content. While some overlap is good, some professors may continue to teach the same content regardless of the course title and fail to take responsibility for an important content/skill area. Too many leadership education programs contain extreme content overlap and the students have gaps in their knowledge base.

At the doctoral course level, the content and knowledge base should extend well beyond the six *Educational Leadership Policy Standards* basic knowledge/skill level to greater academic emphasis on reflective leadership, systems theories, research methods, program evaluation, planning theories and processes, and advanced survey methods. In addition, the doctoral degree plan will include courses in educational economics/cost effectiveness, social and educational policy, future studies and global change, information technologies, and organizational communication.

Assumption Ten: Feedback is continually sought to enhance the teaching and learning. Faculty will conduct annual reviews with graduates serving in leadership roles about the value their graduate experience in guiding them in school improvement. An annual online questionnaire will be created to survey former students about the value of courses taught, relevance of research methods in analyzing school data, and other graduate experiences that have proven valuable to daily practice as school leaders or professors. The questionnaire could be adapted from the one administered by Hoyle and Torres in their 2007 study of top ranked doctoral programs. (See Step Six.)

THE SIX STEPS

The remainder of this book invites the reader to ascend six steps to preparing quality principals and superintendents. As a reminder to the reader, we have attempted to present what we believe to be the state-of-the-art in leadership education for preparing school principals and superintendents.

Our belief is strengthened by our hard work in our own programs, observing numerous programs as visiting professors, serving as external reviewers for ranked and unranked programs, conducting research on the preparation-performance dilemmas, and knowing the research literature on leadership education. Most of all we are driven by the desire to enhance the image of the professional discipline of educational administration and assist our colleagues in their exciting life's work. The six steps are as follows:

1. Selecting the very best students.
2. Pretesting entering master's and doctoral students.

3. Aligning master's degree programs with the *2008 ISSLC Educational Leadership Policy Standards* and doctoral degree programs with the canons of research and best practices.
4. Creating and maintaining effective student advisory committees.
5. Creating and maintaining an effective support staff.
6. Conducting annual program reviews with graduates serving as principals or superintendents.

2

Step One

Selecting the Best and Brightest Students

To be sure, little has been examined in an empirical way concerning educational administration programming and selecting the best talent to become principals and superintendents. Murphy and Vriesenga (2006) suggest future research should attend to aspects that reflect effective preparation programs for school leaders and furthermore give greater attention to outcomes such as student satisfaction, knowledge and application, influence on organization, and of course student productivity. We take from this an urgency to probe the realm of student selection within education leadership preparation programs and moreover, as Murphy and Vriesenga argue, advance toward "[establishing] a collective agenda around the training and education function" (192).

Therefore, in step one, we continue addressing the need for improved scholarship in leadership education programs, wading through the accountability issues, political and ideological differences that impact schools, and focus on the need to recruit and to select prospective students who embrace change and diversity and end with recommended criteria for admission to master's and doctoral degree and licensure programs.

Policies aimed at reforming education in general have encountered many struggles, however. Many good intentioned policies exhibiting potential tend to experience abbreviated life spans making it nearly impossible for systems to achieve any semblance of consistency and continuity. In the past, proposed reforms to the system have generally occurred in piecemeal fashion. While periodic modifications, such as increased rigor on a certification examination, appeared to convey a commitment to improve the quality of public education, the core practices of schooling have remained relatively intact (Elmore 1996; Murphy 2006).

In reality, few compelling incentives exist in the present system for any dramatic change to occur. Because the research on leadership preparation and the link to school improvement is limited in breadth and scope, the indicators by which success is measured still remain diffuse and overall disjointed despite efforts to unify the field (e.g., ISLLC and AASA standards).

Scholars in general acknowledge the need for improved scholarship around leadership education preparation. The landscape of education leadership programming is changing. As Murphy, Moorman, and McCarthy (2008) suggest, the area of educational preparation has become a far more contested policy domain. For instance, states such as Michigan and South Dakota have moved to deregulating educational leadership programs, thus eliminating the provision for certification.

Other states have moved in an opposite direction and have increased oversight over the quality of leadership preparation programs. Consequently, as Murphy and colleagues note, professors in the field of leadership preparation have begun to respond. Much can be learned from prior efforts to improve education. A classic example is Lee and Smith's (1999) study of 30,000 inner-city Chicago schoolchildren. The study found the degree of social support to be positively associated with academic performance but strongest when schools possessed high degrees of academic press.

The evidence suggests that while external support is critical, the collective emphasis on academic excellence proved to be the most pivotal factor. As for designing leadership programming, the implication is that a mere adjustment to the selection process will likely not guarantee immediate results. Real change will demand a mixture of factors that are likely to play out in different ways.

Thus, it is important that the aims and basis for revamping any element of leadership preparation be clearly conveyed. Equally important is whether sufficient capacity by way of intellectual, fiscal, cultural, and political resources is available for these changes to come to fruition (Cohen, Moffitt, & Goldin 2007). The political motives underlying reform are complex and vague. As mentioned previously, many reforms project the illusion of real change but seldom does it translate into student productivity.

The accountability movement, as one example of leveraged change, has forced schools to shift away from the stance of business as usual. Some costs, however, have been exacted by the recent emphasis on student and system production such as narrowing of curricula and more rote instruction. In the current results-driven culture, there is always assumed risk in pushing for leadership preparation reform that falls well short of conferring reasonable benefit and support for performance demands. To meet these demands and expectations, school systems must be given ample support to mitigate these circumstances. In many cases, the support does not exist.

FINDING COMMITTED STUDENTS

Finding students who are committed to these new requirements of the profession is not an easy task. While preferences for the ideal educational leadership student range from program to program, current demands in schools require a new set of skills and knowledge. Saint Louis University, for instance, committed to preparing leaders to deal with complex problems, work collaboratively, manage projects, and to be knowledgeable of school improvement (Everson 2009). Yet, even recognizing that leaders require these skills does not assure that these skills will be applied and work effectively in every setting.

Within any school improvement agenda, a good faith assumption exists that causes will lead to their effects (Hargreaves & Fullan 1998; Hill & Celio 1998). In truth, schools are dynamic organizations that act and rely upon uncertain knowledge. Thus, to truly ascertain success or failure among reforms is problematic because we know that school principals trained in the same program may actually apply their knowledge and skills in entirely different ways depending on culture, demands, and politics. Developing a rubric to evaluate leadership preparation is a formidable challenge given the complexity of schools.

Political and ideological differences often interfere with the primary functions of schooling and hamper good judgment (Simola 1998). According to Cuban (2001), disagreement as to what schools need to become high achieving will be inevitable, but core beliefs in every school, regardless of the circumstances, should continuously pursue high academic standards, highly competent teachers, and a high level of parent involvement. Despite these difficulties, few would object that greater attention should be afforded to leadership aspects that undoubtedly exert influence on the core aspects of schooling. Above all, encouraging and selecting talented committed students to enter the world of school leadership remains a major challenge for professors of educational administration.

What makes student recruitment and selection a much-needed area of examination is the notable lack of scientific inquiry and evidence to support one or several models of best practice. The steps recommended in step one derive from a combination of resources, chiefly our scholarly contributions and those of other distinguished observers, as well as archival data gathered from the very best leadership programs in the country. It is our intention to provide readers a framework from which to critically reflect on current student selection practices and in certain cases completely redesign the process to meet current needs and demands in schools. For that reason, information and recommended practices have been clustered by dimensions or themes identified as critical in our, as well as other scholars' research.

These themes can be used to stimulate discussion and in some instances provide initial structure toward reconceptualizing the student selection process. These themes include (a) a more refined and focused recruitment strategy, (b) publicizing the program to reflect new demands and market forces, (c) a more rigorous admission process that selects students that demonstrate an extraordinary commitment to all students achieving their very best as well as those that exhibit potential as effective managers of information and people, and (d) the search for talented servant school leaders.

Recruitment

The demands placed on school leaders are greater than ever before. In addition to the typical slate of management responsibilities, many are calling for school leaders to have skills and expertise over domains not traditionally associated with programs of administration such as curriculum and instruction (Spillane, Diamond, & Jita 2003), culture and language (Dimmock & Walker 2000), social work (Epstein 1995), and social equity and justice (Scheurich & Skrla 2003; Brown 2004; Shields 2004).

Despite the obvious shift away from traditional managerial training, Hallinger and Snidvongs (2008) argue that while leaders must be ready to inspire and lead, they must also be ready to supervise within a complex and highly uncertain system of rules and roles. As Hallinger and Snidvongs suggest, there tends to be a striking similarity between business curricula and educational administration curricula with respect to a knowledge foundation, the recognition of the increasing global demands, problem solving, ethical awareness, leadership, and other features. It however departs in curricular aspects when dealing with curricular objectives such as "managing information" and "managing competencies."

Also, to manage information, Hallinger and Snidvongs suggest it is "highly simplistic to believe that only the capacity to define the right ends of schooling is sufficient for the schools of the twenty-first century. Despite the strong reaction among many educators against *managerialism*, [the authors] believe that strengthening *management knowledge and skills* is essential if *leaders* are to achieve the vision that they and others define for their schools" (2008, 26).

Striking a balance between selecting the right candidates, preparing them to lead social change, and teaching them effective management techniques and strategies can be difficult and adversarial, especially when values and beliefs collide. One means to achieving the balance is attracting and recruiting students committed to excelling at multiple but sometimes competing dimensions of leadership.

Prospective Students Who Embrace Change and Diversity

To begin, it is important to stress that as a nonnegotiable requirement, prospective students of educational leadership programs must commit to leading school systems that are increasingly populated and diverse. Data provided through the National Center for Education Statistics (NCES) indicate schools will see increases in students over the next decade, particularly children of color. Projections to the year 2017 show the student population in public schools will grow yearly, resulting in an estimated increase of 10 percent between 2005 and 2017 (NCES, nces.ed.gov/fastfacts/display.asp?id=65). Regions in the West, Midwest, and South will experience much of this growth in student enrollment (NCES, nces.ed.gov/programs/projections/projections2017/sec1a.asp).

The ethnic profile of U.S. schools is changing dramatically. Students of other racial groups accounted for 44 percent of the entire student population in 2007—an increase of 22 percent since 1972 (NCES, nces.ed.gov/programs/coe/list/index.asp). Scholars from varying epistemologies are calling for considerable change in how we select and prepare future administrators. From a social justice point of view, the current system inadequately prepares administrators to cope and manage effectively in times of great demographic and cultural change. Obiakor (2006) raises concerns that current preparation of school personnel in general fails to prepare them to be successful in diverse settings.

In 1988, Barbara Jackson, a pioneer in educational leadership, recommended integrating social sciences and humanities to enrich the preparation experiences of school leaders for the increasing number of children of color in schools (cited in Griffiths et al. 1988). She offered this remark in relation to preparation of leaders with regard to supporting the experiences of African American students:

> In order to gain an understanding of the historical-cultural context and a perspective on the status of African Americans over the years, the preparation programs should place a greater emphasis on the social sciences . . . [for instance], when we apply [the concept of culture] to the study of African Americans, we can begin to appreciate how and why certain adaptive behaviors have lasted so long. Slavery lasted two hundred years and was followed by a civil war, a short period of reconstruction, and then another

> hundred years of legal segregation. If approximately thirty years represents a generation, then about ten generations survived under adverse conditions while fighting to gain access to the rights and privileges of the dominant society (312–313).

We draw from this observation a need for prospective students to fully comprehend the magnitude of what is needed from educational leaders today. Jackson, too, concedes management should remain a cornerstone of leadership preparation but argues that the new cadre of leaders must also have the capacity to recognize and act upon social conditions that encompass race, culture, wealth, and other indicators.

Prospective Students Must Embrace the Challenge of Managing Complex Systems

Leaders must be prepared to manage within organizational contexts within which the primary technologies (teaching and learning) are highly uncertain, ritualistic, and idiosyncratic. Unlike supervisors of factories that can anticipate moderate to high levels of consistency, school leaders enjoy much less control over how and what it produces. Historically, schools have operated in what can best be described as a "loosely coupled" system (Weick 1976, 44). The loosely coupled relationship exists between the technical activities of schools (i.e., teaching and learning) and authority (i.e., administration). Teachers consequently enjoy a greater degree of independence and discretion to adapt to uncertain conditions than their factory counterparts.

In addition to the loose coupling, school leaders must conduct their affairs in conditions where tasks and other activities are largely institutionalized and embedded. As Meyer and Rowan (1983) argue, schools are made up of ritual activities and classifications that have attained a level of unquestioned legitimacy over time. For instance, elements of schooling, such as minimum requirements on standardized test performance, minimum credits for graduation, and compulsory attendance, are seldom challenged.

These ritualized classifications engender a "logic of confidence" or an assumption from upper levels of administration that lower levels are abiding by the rituals. Meyer (1986) refers to such a system as an orderly legal environment. Yet, when attempts are made to more tightly control schools (i.e., changes in law and policy), disorders ensue forcing schools to respond. Current trends in schooling point to greater regulation over school outcomes by way of test results and perhaps greater deregulation over certification and licensure. Future leaders must be prepared to accept uncertainty as a normal and enduring characteristic of schools.

Rigorous Selection Criteria and Requirements

In general, programs rely on similar criteria to accept students into school leadership programs. These criteria may consist of standardized scores on examinations such as the GRE and the Miller Analogies Test (MAT), number of years experience as a teacher in the classroom or serving in a leadership capacity, undergraduate grade point average, a statement of purpose or philosophy, and reference letters from supervisors or former professors.

Interviews can often be conducted as they are at institutions such as the University of North Carolina at Chapel Hill. Other institutions are developing performance-based criteria as a way to create a more comprehensive evaluation of the candidate. The University of Texas, for instance, requires applicant portfolios and site visits (i.e., "job embedded observations") in addition to the traditional indicators (epc.edb.utexas.edu/education/departments/edadmin/programs/pselp/areas/principalship/admissions/requirements/).

In regard to statements or philosophy, programs such as the University of Wisconsin–Madison explicitly list the information that students should address within the narrative, such as the administrative or functional areas of interest, career pursuits, and a rationale as to how participation in the program will advance professional and leadership ambitions (www.education.wisc.edu/elpa/admissions/general_adm.html). By and large, the selection criteria for the exemplary leadership programs previously referenced and other notable programs such as the Ohio State University and the Pennsylvania State University are remarkably similar in requirements and expectations.

Between these programs, several attributes are widely shared regarding seeking ideal students. First, schools are searching for students that have assumed key roles in change and improvement. Schools long for servant-type leaders who have exhibited a pattern of selfless service to the school and community. While prior leadership experience or engagement in change or improvement is certainly not a requirement in every program, it does reflect a greater likelihood that the individual will benefit to a greater degree from the knowledge gained in courses.

It will undoubtedly enhance the students' capacity to reflect on his or her leadership in uncertain times, provide valuable points of reference that contextualize course knowledge, stimulate critical discussion and argument over leadership style and approaches, and encourage diversity of thought and viewpoint. Second, schools want to attract students that have intellectual strengths in scholarship and practice.

Given the reliance on standardized examinations such as the GRE and MAT, the implication is such that students will encounter rigorous learning experiences. Unlike prescriptive approaches to learning a discipline, the content in educational leadership programs today is far more reflective, open-ended, contemplative, abstract, and complex. Students will be expected to acquire and analyze data, compose written narrative in a meaningful and thoughtful way, verbally convey ideas and thoughts clearly and articulately, draw data driven conclusions, and link knowledge to practice. Most programs require at least a 1,000 as a combined score on the verbal and quantitative portions of the GRE.

Third, programs rely on indicators that identify students intrinsically motivated to excel and pursue leadership roles to improve the learning experiences for all children. Recommendations from supervisors, professors, and coworkers provide one such indicator that gauges the candidate's commitment to teaching and learning. From the realm of practice, feedback solicited from supervisors who are either principals or central office administrators provides one estimate of the student's commitment to practice and probable success as a leader.

Recommendations can yield information about the candidate's social skills, teaching ability and performance in classroom, attitude, commitment to equity and social justice, and a number of other critical variables. Based on collected data from programs, a minimum of three letters of recommendation should be sought.

Finally, interviews should be conducted to substantiate and validate all other indicators. Face-to-face meetings can often reveal weaknesses and strengths not captured through other indicators. On occasion, prospective students who demonstrate less promise in other areas might be more apt to demonstrate skills and potential in a highly interactive and interpersonal format. In truth, some students simply perform better in these situations. Interviews can occur in a variety of different formats to be sure.

Advances in technology allow for highly interactive experiences without the cost or burdens that accompany travel and time away. Computer programs such as Skype that are virtually free of cost to the user allow for unlimited face-to-face conversations over the computer. Clearly, technology can and should be maximized further in the student selection process. Be that as it may, programs should still base the candidate's evaluation on the totality of the criteria.

Marketing Program to Prospective Students

The movement for change in how we select and prepare educational leaders is building momentum and is coming from new sources. Although pressure for change has traditionally sprung from profession and policy, changes in the environment are forcing leadership preparation programs to take notice. Evaluating aspects relative to student selection and other programming aspects has not occurred broadly across the field. As Glasman, Cibulka, and Ashby (2002) note, the degree at which market forces alter the supply and demand relationship between program providers and student consumers is not easily understood.

Schools are forced to make hard choices, for instance, between accepting marginal but willing students or facing cuts in budgets. Ironically however, leadership programs have stayed the same. Online based institutions, such as the University of Phoenix, are but a few examples of entrepreneurialism in a market otherwise controlled by nonprofit organizations (Glasman et al. 2002). One other incentive to change is the aging leadership presently in the schools and also a diminishing pool of qualified school leaders completing educational leadership programs.

Job demands and pressures, as well as weak financial incentives, push many away. Also Glasman and colleagues contend that preparation programs must be willing and committed to thoughtful change and hold themselves to modeling the tenets. To this end, programs must acknowledge (and in some cases act upon) market changes and subsequently map out a strategy to cope and respond to sudden shifts or trends. Increasing deregulation and a growing cottage industry of leadership preparation programs are forces that can no longer be dismissed or ignored.

As indicated previously, there is a general perception (true or not) that admission standards in leadership education programs are inadequate. And too little effort is made to target women and minorities for inclusion or "to identify individuals interested in working in high needs rural or urban environments" (Hale & Moorman 2003, 9.) This oversight was first mentioned by Mitchell and McSpadden (1977). They admonished departments of educational administration because they found no special admissions policy for minority persons and little concern about the offensiveness of social injustice.

In addition they challenged the departments "to commit themselves to the development of a culturally pluralistic society through the use of available institutional means" (Mitchell and McSpadden 1977, 25). These admonishments by more voices calling for social justice in admitting and preparing a more diverse number of graduates have resulted in positive increases in the numbers of women and minority candidates in leadership education throughout the nation. Selecting the best students with the potential to become exemplary school principals and superintendents is paramount to the success of schools in the United States.

For too long, admission into leadership education graduate programs was either hit-or- miss student self-selection or admissions committees admitting all applicants. This broken system is slowly being replaced by more definitive and proven selection criteria. Only those students with the desire and attributes to become successful school leaders should be encouraged to apply for admission.

We suggest that graduate leadership programs select selfless and diplomatic candidates for leadership preparation. Thus, this step includes the latest research and best practices focused on selection criteria; second, we suggest the best interview questions and reference check procedures that enhance other selection criteria; and third, we suggest informal social activities that provide information about the interpersonal skills of the candidates.

Faculty admissions teams should seek candidates with a proven track record of leading with heart and soul and evidence of skills in communicating and influencing policy to promote equity and justice for all children. These children and youth need candidates guided by selfless and spiritual gifts who can communicate these traits in influencing policy makers. Spiritualist Deepak Chopra believes that schools need leaders who grow from "inside out." This spiritual dimension of leadership is a good omen for future school leaders to help create learning communities that make every attempt to adjust the school and school system to assure that all children become successful, ethical individuals.

To lack the capacity to care about a child's failure in school or to ignore students' background or family circumstances is spiritless administration. Research and close observation has led us to conclude that the most successful principals and superintendents are caring, respect themselves, and are forgiving of others and themselves. Also they are selfless, ethical, enthusiastic, and visionary. The most important task of professors in the student recruiting process is to find future administrators who can create a positive school culture for all students. It is important that admissions criteria include a candidate's record of success in various leadership capacities (i.e., teaching, community, civic groups).

Extra consideration should be given to candidates who have served as leaders in school and community projects, tutoring children and adults, serving the impoverished and elderly, and others in need. Successful school leaders are tireless workers in the schools and community leadership roles. This pattern of service to others begins early in a person's life and continues throughout a professional career as a school leader. Those in a unique position to identify potential school leaders include school principals, superintendents, classroom teachers, counselors, coaches, band directors, and graduate and undergraduate professors.

We believe information about candidates' behavior and interpersonal skills is a stronger predictor of success. Other selection criteria include GRE or MAT scores and grade point averages. While research and opinions differ about the predictability of GRE and MAT scores, our experience tells us that students who score over 500 on the verbal scores on the GRE and over

450 on the MAT are better writers and appear to complete the dissertation with less difficulty. However, high scores may not be enough. For example, applicants scoring below 1,000 on the verbal, math, or analytical portions of the exam, but show promise in other areas, may be admitted.

Other relevant criteria may include reference letters from former and current employers and professors and a writing sample or a personal philosophy statement. While letters from former or current employing principals and superintendents reveal the candidate's work habits and interpersonal skills, letters from former professors provide information about the academic skills and potential for completing a more advanced degree. We find that interview questions often reveal patterns of selfless service and respect people from diverse cultures and ethnic backgrounds. The following interview questions are suggested to assist faculty committees in selecting the selfless leaders into master's and doctoral leadership education programs.

1. What is an example of your servant leadership to an individual or group?
2. What is the most recent project or activity for which you provided team or group leadership?
3. When have you intervened into a situation where a person was being treated unfairly? If so, what action did you take?
4. What is social justice? Talk about a school situation where you applied it.
5. What are you currently reading (i.e., books, articles, or web)?
6. Give an example where you may have bent a rule to help an individual or group.
7. When was the last time you demonstrated diplomacy in solving a problem?
8. How have you handled stressful situations involving two or more people? Give an example.
9. How would you as principal or superintendent create a student-centered school or district to assure that all students will succeed?
10. Recall a situation when a teacher under your leadership was not measuring up to your high standards and expectations for higher student performance. What did you do to help him or her improve teaching practices?

These and similar questions are intended to bring out the interpersonal and team leadership skills of each candidate. The intent is to bring out actual examples of exemplary leadership under stressful situations. Following is a composite of admissions criteria for a master's degree in educational administration followed by a composite of admission criteria for a doctoral degree.

SELECTED ADMISSION CRITERIA FOR A MASTER'S DEGREE IN EDUCATIONAL ADMINISTRATION

The following suggested admissions criteria are similar in most programs, but the ways in which they are applied in the process can vary. We want to emphasize the need to identify potential school administrators who have a passion to educate all children, through a solid record of service that exemplifies social justice. While intellect is still important, graduate programs should give stronger consideration to candidates with the heart for leadership. Thus, we suggest the following admissions criteria and processes for selecting aspiring principals and superintendents.

Recommended Criteria for Admission to the Master's Degree Program

The following criteria are a composite selected from the following master's degree program materials: Drexel University, Idaho State University, Sam Houston State University, Ohio State University, Texas A&M University, and the University of North Texas.

Purpose

The Master's degree in educational administration is designed to increase the student's understanding, knowledge, and skills in core professional studies and educational leadership directly linked to building level administration.

Criteria for Admission

1. A bachelor's degree from an accredited institution.
2. Undergraduate grade point average of 3.0 or higher for all upper division credits.
3. GRE score at the 35th percentile or above on one of the sections (i.e., verbal, quantitative, analytical).
4. Three letters of recommendation—professional and academic. The recommendation forms should ask the recommender to focus on applicant's talent and heart to become a successful school leader. Signed letters must be submitted in a sealed envelope signed across the flap by the recommender.
5. A two- to three-page essay by the applicant discussing why he or she is interested in pursuing the master's degree.
6. Conduct a fifteen- to twenty-minute interview using selected questions from those listed previously.

7. Supply official transcripts from all universities and colleges and other postsecondary educational institutions attended. Students may supply official electronic transcripts directly to university admissions.
8. Submit admission forms and application fee to the Office of Graduate Studies, and be admitted by the Office of Graduate Studies.
9. International students must submit a Test of English as a Foreign Language (TOEFL) score of 550 for paper and computer based or 79 for Internet based test, Michigan English Language Battery (MELAB) minimum score of 82, or International English Language Testing System (IELTS) minimum score of 7. Any one of these is required of an applicant from another country where the native language is not English, unless a bachelor's degree or its equivalent was earned in a country where English is the native language.

Admission Process

1. The applicant may submit either paper application or electronic application. Application materials are available from the Graduate Department of Educational Leadership or the Office of Graduate Studies. International application materials are available at the International Student Admissions office and can be downloaded online.
2. Applicants must submit the following application materials to the Office of Graduate Studies.
3. The application materials are sent to the Department of Educational Leadership and are reviewed for completeness and acceptability. If the application is complete, the department faculty will recommend the applicant be accepted as classified, conditional, or rejected based on the required criteria.

Notification of Admission

1. Applicants will be notified of their acceptance or rejection via a letter from the Department of Educational Leadership or the Office of Graduate Studies (depending on current operations).
2. The acceptance notice will include information materials, as well as, an advisor assignment.

RECOMMENDED CRITERIA FOR ADMISSION TO AN ED.D. OR PH.D. IN EXECUTIVE LEADERSHIP

The criteria are a composite of doctoral program materials from Ohio State University, Seton Hall University, Teachers College, Columbia University, the University of Tennessee, the University of Nebraska, Drexel University, Sam Houston State University, Texas A&M University, and the University of Wisconsin–Madison.

Purpose

The Doctoral Program is designed for those individuals who aspire to school district leadership. The program combines the practical and theoretical study of organizational behavior, learning theories and applications, community dynamics, educational policy, law, politics, and accountability with attention to four cross-cutting themes—diversity, technology, visionary leadership, and organizational change. In addition the programs include various research methods to prepare the candidate for an academic career.

Suggested Criteria for Admission

1. A master's degree in educational administration or related field.
2. A superior academic record, including two transcripts from all previous colleges attended excluding this one. One copy should be sent to the Graduate Admissions Office and the other to the Department of Educational Administration. Benchmark undergraduate grade point average is 3.00 in the last sixty hours and 3.50 (4-point scale) for the master's degree.
3. Recent scores (within the last five years) on the GRE or the MAT that indicate potential for success in doctoral level work. Some programs require a GRE score of 1,600 or a MAT score of 50. In a few programs applicants with an undergraduate and graduate grade point average of 3.50 are not required to take the GRE or MAT.
4. A resume outlining previous education and professional history.
5. A statement of personal and professional goals.
6. Submission of a scholarly writing sample (not exceeding three pages) is based on one of the suggested doctoral questions in Step Two of this book; or, the faculty at the University of Wisconsin offers an assessment process to determine the overall writing skill of the applicant. The applicants will address the following questions in an essay that does not exceed three pages. The questions are as follows:
   1. What are the primary personal and career goals you have identified as important for your intellectual and professional advancement over the next five to ten years?
   2. In what ways will these goals be advanced through a doctoral program at UW–Madison?

3. As you will note, we are interested in developing and maintaining a diverse and engaging learning community. Please identify any unique or special contributions you will bring to this community.

Faculty members grading the essays follow the following guidelines to help determine the quality level of the writing.

A "Strong" essay is characterized by:

a. A clear, thorough, well-organized essay that expresses ideas in a detail and engaging manner.
b. Addresses all components of the instructions.
c. Paragraphs signal the divisions of thought and sentences flow with ideas in a logical sequence.
d. No (very few) noticeable errors in composition.
e. The articulation of clear scholarly interests that are consistent with the department's mission and that may expand knowledge within the field.

A "Satisfactory" essay is characterized by:

a. A detailed, well-organized essay.
b. Addresses all components of the instructions.
c. Paragraphs signal the major divisions of thought and sequence.
d. Few errors in composition.
e. The articulation of scholarly interests that are consistent with the department's vision, and mission.

A "Weak" essay is characterized by:

a. A well-organized but insufficiently detailed essay.
b. Addresses some, but not all, of the components of the instructions.
c. Paragraphs do not contain main topics.
d. A distracting number of errors in composition.
e. No articulation of scholarly interests

7. Three letters of recommendation: At least one letter should be from a professor who is able to determine if the applicant can do scholarly writing and research.
8. An interview with three faculty members. The eight doctoral entry-level questions found in step two provided to the applicants at least two weeks before the interview. The interview committee would then select three of the questions found in step two of this book.

9. TOEFL (minimum score of 550 on paper or 213 computer-based or 79 Internet test), MELAB (minimum 82), or IELTS (minimum 7) is required of an applicant from another country where the native language is not English, unless a bachelor's degree or its equivalent was earned in a country where English is the native language.
10. All applicants to the Executive Ph.D./Ed.D. program must serve or have served in a K–12 campus or school district as a practicing administrator for at least one year to be considered for the program.

Notification of Admission

All admissions decisions are made by the program/department faculty as a whole after the application deadline. Accordingly students are admitted to the certification program three times a year; students are admitted to the master's degree program twice each year; and students are admitted to the Executive Leadership doctoral program only once each calendar year.

No application will be considered for admission to any program unless all documentation is on file. A favorable vote of the program/department faculty is required for the department to recommend admission to the graduate school. Upon admission, a member of the faculty of the program will be assigned as the initial advisor. This admission statement was developed by the Department of Educational Leadership and Policy Analysis at the University of Wisconsin, Madison, Wisconsin and is very similar to other recognized programs in educational administration.

CRITERIA FOR STUDENTS APPLYING FOR ADMINISTRATIVE LICENSURE ONLY

The following material comes from the School of Educational Policy and Leadership in the College of Education and Human Ecology at Ohio State University.

This is a well-designed comprehensive licensure program for the state of Ohio and is very adaptable to other states requiring the NCATE/ISLLC 2008 or similar standards.

Instructions

Applicants who already have a master's degree may obtain an administrative license without completing a second degree. The following are criteria for admission to the Self-Paced Licensure Program for School Principals:

1. Three letters of recommendation.
2. One-page statement of interest in the principalship.

3. Resume.
4. Bachelor's degree with a minimum 3.0 grade point average (original transcripts for all coursework).
5. Licensure application form.

The following are criteria for admission to the Accelerated Program for Principals:

1. Nomination letter from district superintendent.
2. Two additional letters of recommendation.
3. Nomination form signed by the district superintendent.
4. One page statement of interest in the principalship.
5. Resume.
6. Bachelor's degree with a minimum combined 3.0 grade point average (original transcripts for all course work).
7. Licensure application form.

The following are criteria for admission to the Accelerated Licensure Program for Superintendents:

1. Nomination letter from district superintendent.
2. Two additional letters of recommendation.
3. Nomination form by district superintendent.
4. One-page statement of interest in the superintendency.
5. Resume.
6. Bachelor's degree with a minimum combined 3.0 grade point average (original transcripts for all course work).
7. Master's degree with a minimum 3.0 grade point average.
8. Copy of principal license or certificate.
9. Licensure application form.

For greater detail including course work and internships required in this excellent licensure program at Ohio State University go to ere.osu.edu/epl.

In concluding step one, we urge our readers to renew their efforts in identifying diverse cohorts of talented, energetic candidates who lead with heart and are proven team-oriented classroom teachers, coaches, music directors, club sponsors, and leaders in community activities and organizations.

To be sure, the recommended admission criteria gathered from numerous programs is mainly representative of the canons of traditional educational leadership programming. The criteria derive in part from our body of work, experience, and professional judgment. The criteria can be adjusted to fit programs of all size and type. Step Two details how to assess entry-level knowledge and experiences of the students accepted into your programs.

3

Step Two

Pretesting Entering Master's and Doctoral Students

After admitting the students, we remind readers about the first tenet toward excellence in teaching: find out the students' entry-level knowledge in educational leadership. Our observations made us very aware that this vital assessment step is overlooked in most leadership education program in the United States and Canada.

Thus, this second step introduces the LSI to access the entry-level knowledge and participation levels of the beginning master's degree students and a higher level essay examination for entering doctoral students. As presented in Step One, similar admission processes used across the nation for the master's degree include traditional criteria (i.e., grade point average, GRE or MAT scores, an interview, and or a writing sample).

The standard admissions criteria for most doctoral degree programs is an acceptable grade point average in previous graduate work, acceptable GRE or MAT scores, recommendations from former employers and professors, a structured interview, and either a writing sample about a critical policy or leadership issue or an oral presentation about similar big topics. However, these data are often discarded after the students are accepted into the program.

Thus, we urge faculty members to use the LSI and conduct a knowledge inventory of each new master's degree student based on established standards that represent the minimum core knowledge base. Also, we recommend using the more advanced essay questions to assess the knowledge base about higher order cognition for new doctoral students.

Therefore, we recommend that the entering master's degree candidate complete the LSI that includes the thirty-one functions linked to the six broader standards from the *Educational Leadership Standards: ISLLC 2008* or related standards preferred in some states. As indicated previously, the LSI is created to assist professors in gathering data on the extent of each student's entry-level skills and participation in the thirty-one skills and functions.

Entering doctoral students need not take the LSI since most of them would be licensed school principals and have passed the state exam. Thus, entering doctoral students would respond in writing to questions about advanced research topics (i.e., crises in U.S. education, impact of school leaders on student achievement, inequities in schooling, economics of education, education policy, and organizational theories).

While critics claim that the ISLLC standards are merely shallow measures of the knowledge base, they are nonetheless minimum benchmarks for the vast majority of university and alternative preparation programs and state licensure examinations.

The ISLLC standards recently revised are now the *Educational Leadership Policy Standards: ISLLC* (2008) and are compatible with the NCATE and the ELCC standards.

We propose that entry-level master's degree students complete the following LSI to assist faculty in assessing students' mastery or accomplishment level for each of the thirty-one leadership functions in the 2008 *Educational Leadership Policy Standards: ISLLC.* In addition, the test results will guide faculty in diagnosing the knowledge gaps among the candidates and prescribing course work and independent studies to bring all students to the highest knowledge levels. Most entry-level students will have very limited participation in the thirty-one functions. There may be some exceptions if a beginning student has been engaged as a teacher leader or a member of the site-based decision-making committee.

Following the LSI, the reader will find six challenging questions for doctoral students that extend beyond the knowledge base in the LSI. Students' written responses to the questions will assist faculty advisors and committees in guiding students into specific independent studies and courses to close knowledge gaps and enrich students' intellectual experiences.

LEADERSHIP SKILLS INVENTORY

Instructions

Each master's degree student will complete the following skills inventory by placing a circle around their levels of mastery or participation in each of the thirty-one leadership functions linked to the six 2008 *Educational Leadership Policy Standards: ISLLC.*

Standard 1

An education leader promotes the success of every student by facilitating the development, articulation, implementation, and stewardship of a vision of learning that is shared and supported by all stakeholders.

Functions What is the extent of your participation in the following leadership functions? I have participated in each function (3) *extensively*, (2) *moderately*, or (1) *very little*. Circle the appropriate number after each statement. As an educator I . . .

A. Collaborate in developing and implementing a shared vision and mission 3 2 1
B. Collect and use data to identify goals, assess organizational effectiveness, and promote organizational learning 3 2 1
C. Create and implement plans to achieve goals....3 2 1
D. Promote continuous and sustainable improvement 3 2 1
E. Monitor and evaluate progress and revise plans....3 2 1

Standard 2

An education leader promotes the success of every student by advocating, nurturing, and sustaining a school culture and instructional program conducive to student learning and staff professional growth.

Functions As an educator I have participated in each function (3) *extensively*, (2) *moderately*, or (1) *very little*. Circle the appropriate number after each statement. As an educator I . . .

A. Nurture and sustain a culture of collaboration, trust, learning, and high expectations for all students....3 2 1
B. Create a comprehensive, rigorous, and coherent curricular program 3 2 1
C. Create a personalized and motivating learning environment for students....3 2 1
D. Supervise instruction....3 2 1
E. Develop assessment and accountability systems to monitor student progress....3 2 1
F. Develop the instructional and leadership capacity of staff....3 2 1
G. Maximize time spent on quality instruction....3 2 1
H. Promote the use of the most effective and appropriate technologies to support teaching and learning....3 2 1
I. Monitor and evaluate the impact of the instructional program 3 2 1

Standard 3

An education leader promotes the success of every student by ensuring management of the organization, operation, and resources for a safe, efficient, an effective learning environment.

Function As an educator I have participated in each function (3) *extensively*, (2) *moderately*, or (1) *very little*. Circle the appropriate number after each statement. As an educator I . . .

A. Monitor and evaluate the management operation system 3 2 1
B. Obtain, allocate, align, and efficiently utilize human, fiscal, and technological resources 3 2 1
C. Promote and protect the welfare and safety of students and staff 3 2 1
D. Promote the capacity for distributed leadership 3 2 1
E. Ensure teacher and organizational time is focused to support quality instruction and student learning..........3 2 1

Standard 4

An education leader promotes the success of every student by collaborating with the faculty and community members, responding to diverse community interests and needs, and mobilizing community resources.

Functions As an educator I have participated in each function (3) *extensively*, (2) *moderately*, or (1) *very little*. Circle the appropriate number after each statement. As an educator I . . .

A. Collect and analyze data and information pertinent to the educational environment in the school..........3 2 1
B. Promote understanding, appreciation, and use of the community's diverse cultural, social, and intellectual resources..........3 2 1
C. Build and sustain productive relationships with families and care givers..........3 2 1
D. Build and sustain productive relationships with community partners 3 2 1

Standard 5

An education leader promotes the success of every student by acting with integrity, fairness, and in an ethical manner.

Functions As an educator I have participated in each function (3) *extensively*, (2) *moderately*, or (1) *very little*. Circle the appropriate number after each statement. As an educator I . . .

A. Ensure a system of accountability for every student's academic and social success 3 2 1
B. Model principles of self-awareness, reflective practice, transparency, and ethical behavior....................3 2 1
C. Safeguard the values of democracy, equity, and diversity 3 2 1
D. Consider and evaluate the potential moral and ethical consequences of decision making....................3 2 1
E. Promote social justice and ensure that individual student needs inform all aspects of schooling 3 2 1

Standard 6

An education leader promotes the success of every student by understanding, responding to, and influencing the political, social, economic, legal, and cultural context.

Functions As an educator I have participated in each function (3) *extensively*, (2) *moderately*, or (1) *very little*. Circle the appropriate number after each statement. As an educator I . . .

A. Advocate for children, families, and caregivers 3 2 1
B. Act to influence local, district, state, and national decisions affecting student learning....................3 2 1
C. Assess, analyze, and anticipate emerging trends and initiatives in order to adapt leadership strategies....................3 2 1

Participation Level Score _______

LEADERSHIP SKILLS AND KNOWLEDGE INVENTORY FOR ENTRY-LEVEL DOCTORAL STUDENTS

The following questions are suggested for each new doctoral student upon admission to the program. At least two faculty members will grade the responses. Grading is categorized in the following way: E = excellent; G = good; and M = marginal. Students who score an E and G are cleared to begin class with no conditions while the M students are assigned appropriate readings by an advisor who will administer an oral exam before the semester begins. This process can be very valuable for new doctoral students with limited experience in and knowledge of public or private education in the United States.

1. Identify and discuss four major crises in U.S. education and provide possible solutions (5–8 pages).

2. Identify and discuss research underway to discover links between principal and superintendent leadership responsibilities and student academic performance (5–8 pages).
3. Identify inequities in public and private school education and suggest solutions (3–8 pages).
4. Explain how schools are financed and suggest ways to improve the current system (3–6 pages).
5. What education policy would you like to initiate that could lead to a major reform in public education (5–8 pages)?
6. What is the value of organizational theory to practical operation of schools and school districts (4–5 pages)?

The data provided from the LSI for master's students and the six doctoral entry-level questions are very important to the preparation of exemplary school leaders because most graduate programs tend to assume that all entry students share common knowledge and work experience. The recent growth in cohort programs has been beneficial in attracting experienced classroom teachers and beginning administrators with some similar experiences and prior knowledge. There are common skills required for the classroom and assistant principals, but knowledge gaps of aspiring and acting school leaders must be addressed. Assessing the experience and knowledge levels suggested previously can guide the professor in assuring that master's degree students acquire the basic knowledge and skills and can pass the licensure exam that qualifies them to enter their first administrative job.

In addition, faculty advisors to doctoral students will have valuable data on entry-level doctoral students, which can help close knowledge gaps and enhance advanced intellectual development to better prepare them for administrative positions. It is also another measure of the student's writing skills and depth of reflection on critical issues.

4

Step Three

Aligning Master's Degree Programs with the 2008 ISLLC Education Policy Standards *and Doctoral Degree Programs with the Canons of Research and Best Practices*

Following Step Two, the knowledge assessment, Step Three contains two main foci: (a) assist faculty in guiding master's degree students to close knowledge gaps identified by the LSI scores. Thus, readings, curricula, and class projects need to be aligned with the *ISLLC 2008 Leadership Education Policy* standards and functions required for entry-level administration; (b), for entry-level doctoral students we align more advanced readings and projects relevant to the entry essay questions.

These readings and projects are designed to help assure that new doctoral students are prepared to enter their first class. That is, the master's degree is much more prescribed due to state and national standards and licensure requirements, while the doctoral degree rests on these minimum standards and functions. It requires greater depth and reflection to meet the career knowledge and skills required to succeed as superintendents or as policy administrators. While the focus of this book is the preparation of exemplary principals and superintendents for public schools, some doctoral graduates may eventually teach in higher education or fill roles as policy analysts in state or national education agencies. Thus, while the Ed.D. Executive degree is primarily to prepare exemplary school leaders it also prepares the student to teach in higher education if that is their choice in the near future or later in their public school careers.

First, we aligned all course content on the master's degree with the *ISLLC* standards and functions. For this alignment to be successful, faculty must distribute their course syllabi to all colleagues to avoid extreme overlap in course content. This will assure that the six standards and thirty-one related functions are given adequate attention. Second, while much of the doctoral degree program content is related to the six ISLLC/ NCATE standards, the Ed.D. and Ph.D. degree plans reach beyond the master's degree in depth and rigor and place more emphasis on domains of theory, research methods, economic theory, cost accounting, and social and organizational change. Doctoral students' responses to the essay questions will be assessed by advisors, and curriculum decisions will be guided by quality of student responses to the six questions.

Below is a step-by-step plan that repeats each of the six standards and thirty-one functions. We rely on selected readings recommended by an expert panel appointed by the NPBEA. The expert panel collaborated during 2006–2008 with members of the Chief School Officers under the leadership of Joe Simpson, Deputy Director Council of Chief States School Officers, and Richard Flanary, Steering Committee Chair and Director of Professional Development for the NASSP. Also Honor Fede, Special Projects Manager for NASSP, served as the Project Coordinator. The NPBEA expert panel was selected to represent research, policy, and practice of leadership standards.

Their charge was to revise the standards to include skills, knowledge, and best practices of both principals and system administrators other than business managers. In addition, the expert panel was charged to review the most relevant research literature to support the standards and functions (ISLLC 2008 Empirical Research Database Chief State School Officers). We thank the following panel members for their contributions to this supporting research. The panel members are as follows:

- Len Foster, Washington State University
- Mary Gunter, Arkansas Tech University
- John R. Hoyle, Texas A&M University
- Kenneth Leithwood, University of Toronto
- Beryl Levinger, Monterey Institute of International Studies
- Nelda H. Cambron-McCabe, Miami University
- Jerry D. McCausland, Dickenson College
- David Monk, Pennsylvania State University
- Joseph Murphy, Peabody College, Vanderbilt University
- Rosemary Papa, Northern Arizona University
- Nancy Sanders, Council of Chief State School Officers
- Timothy Waters, McREL, Inc.

After thirteen months and several meetings and conference calls, the panel completed its work which was approved by the NPBEA in 2008. After final approval, the *Educational Leadership Policy Standards 2008* were adopted by the NCATE to become their minimum benchmarks for the evaluation of leadership education programs and licensure examinations for aspiring school administrators.

Therefore, these six standards and thirty-one related functions represent the minimum knowledge and skill levels for master's degree students pursuing administrative careers and the follow-up step after administering the LSI found in Step Two. Again, Step Three repeats each standard and related function and includes selected references supporting each standard and function (some of the readings are recommendations by the expert panel). In addition to other readings, we provide course suggestions that closely align with each standard and function and suggest relevant class projects to help students close knowledge and skill gaps and assist faculty in planning course syllabi. This process will not only strengthen class content and delivery but should also enable students to achieve high scores on licensure examinations.

STANDARDS, FUNCTIONS, REFERENCES, CURRICULA, AND CLASS PROJECTS

Standard 1

An education leader promotes the success of every student by facilitating the development, articulation, implementation, and stewardship of a vision of learning that is shared and supported by stakeholders.

Function A

Collaboratively develop and implement a shared vision and mission.

References

1. Waters, J. T., & Marzano, R. J. (2006). *School district leadership that works: The effect of superintendent leadership on student achievement.* Aurora, Colo.: McREL. Conclusions: Five district responsibilities were identified in the research: goal setting processes, goals for achievement and instruction, board agreement with goals, monitoring goals, and use of resources to support goals.
2. Hoyle, J. (2007c). *Leadership and futuring: Making visions happen.* Thousand Oaks, Calif.: Corwin Press. Conclusions: Step-by-step visioning process for each school campus or the entire district. See pages 77–85.
3. Guthrie, J., & Schuermannn, P. (2010). *Successful school leadership: Planning, politics, performance and power.* Boston: Allyn & Bacon. Conclusions: A cutting edge look at strategic planning and assessment of programs.

Curriculum Recommendations The principalship, futurism, and planning or other courses with a unit on visioning and planning.

Project Recommendations The student will write a vision statement for the school and share it with class members and professor. The professor will conduct a visioning activity with class members using exercises found in Hoyle (2007c) *Leadership and futuring*, 75-97.

Function B

Collect and use data to identify goals, assess organizational effectiveness, and promote organizational learning.

References

1. Newman et al. (2001). Instructional program coherence: What is it and why it should guide school improvement policy? *Education evaluation and policy analysis,* 23(4), 297–322. Conclusions: Strong positive relationship found between improving program coherence and student achievement.
2. Knapp et al. (2006). *Data-informed leadership in education.* Seattle: Center for the study of teaching and policy. Conclusions: The report synthesizes, interprets ideas, and sets up frameworks concerning the value and quality of using data to improve instruction.
3. Parkay, W., Hass, G., & Anctil, E. (2010). *Curriculum leadership* (9th ed.). Boston: Allyn & Bacon, 357–412. Conclusions: A through walk through the entire assessment process.
4. Goddard, R., & Skrla, L. (2006). The influence of school social context on teachers' collective efficacy beliefs. *Educational administration quarterly,* 42(2), 216–235. Conclusions: Teachers' perceptions of self-efficacy beliefs about their ability to influence curriculum, instruction and student learning.

Curriculum Recommendations Course in program evaluation, tests and measurements, or instructional management in schools.

Project Recommendations Analyze a school district's student performance data for the past three years in math, reading, science, and social studies. Next ask students to write a three-page overview of their impressions gained from the data.

Function C

Create and implement plans to achieve goals.

References

1. Murphy, J. (1990). Principal instructional leadership. In L. Lotto & P. Thurston (Eds.) *Advances in educational administration: Changing perspec-*

tive on the school, 163–200. Conclusions: Principal leadership is the key to aligning and monitoring achievement goals for all students.

2. Hoyle, J., English, F., & Steffy, B. (1998). *Skills for successful 21st century school leaders.* Lanham, Md.: Rowman & Littlefield Education, chapters 1, 5, and 6. Conclusions: A rich source on strategies to collaborate with teachers in accomplishing goals for student achievement.
3. Scheurich, J. (1998). Highly successful and loving public elementary school populated by low s.e.s. children of color: Core beliefs and cultural characteristics. *Urban Education,* 33(4). 451–491. Conclusions: The fact that these highly successful low income neighborhood schools are academically competitive with—or superior to—other Anglo schools suggest exemplary leadership by the principal.
4. Koschoreck, J. (2001). Accountability and educational equity in the transformation of an urban district. *Education and Urban Society,* 33(3), 284–304. Conclusions: A report of active participation of all stakeholders toward a common goal of success and high achievement for all children.
5. Parkay, F., Hass, G., & Anctil, E. (2010). *Curriculum leadership* (9th ed.). Boston: Allyn & Bacon. Conclusions: An excellent resource on the issue of curriculum planning and goal achievement.

Curriculum Recommendations Course in the principalship, curriculum planning, leadership, special populations, or instructional planning and assessment.

Project Recommendations Design a school-based report that includes student achievement results by class, gender, socioeconomic status, and race. Also, analyze projected student population trends by ethnicity for the next ten years. Develop five recommendations based on the findings.

Function D

Promote continuous and sustainable improvement.

References

1. Badgett, J., & Christmann, E. (2009b). *Designing middle and high school instruction and assessment.* Thousand Oaks, Calif.: Corwin Press. Conclusions: The entire book offers the reader ways to promote continuous and sustainable improvement through using the cognitive domain and testing procedures.
2. Creighton, T. (2001). *Schools and data.* Thousand Oaks, Calif.: Corwin Press. Conclusions: A well-written and understandable book on the use of statistics to promote continuous improvement in schools. He provides a step by step easy to follow guide using existing data to help students.

3. Hoyle, J., English, F., & Steffy, B. (1998). *Skills for successful 21st century school leaders*. Lanham, Md.: Rowman & Littlefield Education, 141–165. Conclusions: A hands-on useful chapter for practitioners charged with solving problems though data gathering and analysis.

Curriculum Recommendations Program evaluation, tests and measurement, and instructional management.

Project Recommendations Apply the CIPP (Context, Input, Process, and Product) or other evaluation model to assess the progress of a math, science, and social studies curriculum with sixth-grade students (i.e., where are the students now, what are the performance objectives, how well are students achieving, and what interventions are needed).

Function E

Monitor and evaluate progress and revise plans.

References

1. Theoharis, G. (2007). Social justice educational leaders and resistance: Toward a theory of social justice leadership. *Educational Administration Quarterly*, 43(2), 221–258. Conclusions: Through enacting social justice, six of seven principals raised student achievement by changing structures, rigor of curriculum, and sound accountability measures.
2. Brown et al. (2004). Student achievement in high performing middle schools and low performing middle schools. *Education and Urban Society*, 36(4), 428–456. Conclusions: Principals in the higher performing schools created a shared vision of high performance and were viewed as experts by faculty who collaborated with him/her to improve their classroom instruction.
3. Wong, K., & Nicotera, A. (2007). *Successful schools and educational accountability*. Boston: Pearson. Conclusions: An excellent account of school accountability and steps to assess effectiveness.
4. Badgett, J., & Christmann, E. (2009a). *Designing elementary instruction and assessment: Using the cognitive domain*. Thousand Oaks, CA: Corwin Press. Conclusions: A groundbreaking book that provides a four-step model (1) content area standards, (2) modified standards, (3) unit plan objectives, and (4) daily instructional objectives in an understandable sequence of increasing specificity.

Curriculum Recommendations Course in program evaluation, leadership and planning, and the principalship or instructional leadership and planning.

Project Recommendations Review the school curriculum to assess whether it focuses on higher-order thinking and problem solving and report findings to class.

Standard 2

An education leader promotes the success of every student by advocating, nurturing, and sustaining a school culture and instructional program conducive to student learning and staff professional growth.

Function A

Nurture and sustain a culture of collaboration, trust, learning, and high expectations.

References

1. Achilles, C. (1999). *Let's put kid's first, finally getting class size right.* Thousand Oaks, CA: Corwin Press. Conclusions: Definitive evidence that smaller classes, especially in the early years, leads to academic success.
2. Hoyle, J. (2002). *Leadership and the force of love: Six keys to motivating with love.* Thousand Oaks, Calif.: Corwin Press. Conclusions: The power of unconditional love expressed by school leaders drives every highly successful school family.
3. Barnett, K., & McCormich, J. (2004). Leadership and individual principal-teacher relationships in schools. *Educational Administration Quarterly,* 40(3), 406–434. Conclusions: Individual concern is a critical element of school leadership: Vision is important but may not be shared by teachers if the concern is missing.
4. Marshall, C., & Oliva, M. (2010). *Leadership for social justice,* (2nd ed.). Boston: Allyn & Bacon. Conclusions: The book is an excellent source to assist school leaders in creating equitable practices for students and faculty.

Curriculum Recommendations Leadership theory and principalship.

Project Recommendations Ask students to design a workable climate plan, and design and administer a "homemade" teacher self-report climate instrument.

Function B

Create a comprehensive, rigorous, and coherent curricular program.

References

1. Sherman, R., & Jones, T. (2008). Curriculum, instruction, and assessment. In J. Vornberg (Ed.). *Texas public school organization and administration*, 324–364. Dubuque, Iowa: Kendall Hunt Publishers. Conclusions: Good overview of curriculum development, organization and implementation.
2. McNeil, J. (1996). *Curriculum: A comprehensive introduction.* Los Angeles: Harper Collins. Conclusions: A big picture of the role of curriculum in creating successful schools and students.
3. Glickman, C., Gordon, S., & Gordon, J. M (2010). *Supervision and instructional leadership* (8th ed.). Boston: Allyn & Bacon. Conclusions: An excellent source for beginning or veteran school leaders attempting to lead teachers to higher performance.

Curriculum Recommendations Instructional leadership, curriculum development, or curriculum theory.

Project Recommendations Plan and deliver an in-service dealing with key concepts related to curriculum alignment, and detail the steps you would take in the redesign of the school's science program.

Function C

Create a personalized and motivating learning environment for students.

References

1. Cruickshank, D., & Haefele, D. (2001). Good teachers, plural. *Educational Leadership*, 58(5), 26–30. Conclusions: Good teachers create a personalized and motivating learning environment.
2. Good, T., & Brophy, J. (1997). *Looking into classrooms* (7th ed.). New York: Addison and Wesley. Conclusions: This book is a classic on classroom management for student learning and motivation.
3. Hoy, A., & Hoy, W. (2006). *Instructional leadership.* Boston: Pearson, 126–204. Conclusions: An on-target look at the key issues around a personalized and motivating learning environment.

Curriculum Recommendations Instructional management, special populations, or instructional theory.

Project Recommendations Report on how to help teachers frame a definition and plan for teacher empowerment, and create an in-service session for classroom teachers dealing with student motivation.

Function D

Supervise Instruction

References

1. Cruickshank, D., & Haefele, D. (2001). Good teachers, plural. *Educational Leadership*, 58(5), 26–30. Conclusions: Good teachers create a personalized and motivating learning environment.
2. Good, T., & Brophy, J. (1997). *Looking into classrooms* (7th ed.). New York: Addison and Wesley. Conclusions: This book is a classic on classroom management for student learning and motivation.
3. Hoy, A., & Hoy, W. (2006). *Instructional leadership*. Boston: Pearson, 126–204. Conclusions: An on-target look at the key issues around a personalized and motivating learning environment.

Curriculum Recommendations Instructional management, special populations, or instructional theory.

Project Recommendations Report on how to help teachers frame a definition and plan for teacher empowerment, and create an in-service session for classroom teachers dealing with student motivation.

Function E

Develop assessment and accountability systems to monitor student progress.

References

1. Wong, K., & Nicotera, A. (2007). *Successful schools and educational accountability*. Boston: Pearson, 130–160. Conclusions: An excellent resource on the issues of accountability systems to monitor student progress.
2. Badgett, J., & Christmann, E. (2009a). *Designing elementary instruction and assessment*. Thousand Oaks, Calif.: Corwin Press. Conclusions: A wonderful reference for any teacher and administrator designing the best testing strategies, especially on writing, short-answer, and essay items, performance-based assessment and portfolios.
3. Badgett, J., & Christmann, E. (2009b). *Designing middle and high school instruction and assessment: Using the cognitive domain*. Thousand Oaks, CA: Corwin Press. Conclusions: An excellent source for developing unit and daily lesson plans for middle and high schools based on state and national content standards and provides detail examples for each level of Bloom's Taxonomy.

Function F

Develop the instructional and leadership capacity of staff.

References

1. Hoy, A., & Hoy, W., (2006). *Instructional leadership: A research based guide to learning in schools*. Boston: Pearson, 1–24 and 168–204. Conclusions:

A well-organized step-by-step look at developing and understanding of the instructional and leadership capacity among staff members.
2. Harris, S., Moore, H., & Farrow, V. (2008). Extending transfer of learning theory to transformative learning theory: A model for promoting teacher leadership. *Theory into Practice,* 47(4), 318–327. Conclusions: An interesting university supervisory program designed to empower teachers to take primary responsibility for guiding and developing future colleagues.
3. Jenlink, P., & Jenlink, K. (2008). Creating democratic learning communities: Transformative work as spatial practice. *Theory into Practice,* 47(4), 311–317. Conclusions: The authors explore what is necessary to transform the social space of schools into democratically practiced places of learning.

Curriculum Recommendations Instructional management, foundations of education, and the prinicipalship.

Project Recommendations After reading the article by Jenlink and Jenlink, ask the students to write down three to four suggestions that they may use to create more democratic learning communities.

Function G

Maximize time spent on quality instruction.

References

1. Good, T. & Brophy, J (1997) *Looking into classrooms* (7th ed.). New York: Addison & Wesley. Conclusions: Every child needs individual time to complete projects.
2. McLeod, J. et al. (2003). *The key elements of classroom management: Managing time and space, student behavior, and instructional strategies.* Alexandria, VA: Association for Supervision and Curriculum Development. Conclusions: Time on task and time for each student to reflect are highlighted.

Curriculum Recommendations Curriculum management and teaching strategies and patterns of learning.

Project Recommendations Ask student to read the works of Benjamin Bloom about student time on task and deliver an oral report.

Function H

Promote the use of the most effective and appropriate technologies to support teaching and learning.

References

1. Wickersham, L. (2008). Texas schools, technology integration, and the twenty-first century. In J. Vornberg (Ed.). *Texas public school organization and administration*, 611–627. Dubuque, IA: Kendall Hunt Publishers. Conclusions: A very thorough overview of the latest applications of technology to classroom learning and its impact on class time and efficiency.
2. Parkay, F., Hass, G., & Anctil, E. (2010). *Curriculum leadership* (9th ed.). Boston: Allyn & Bacon. See chapter 6, "Developing, Implementing, and Evaluating the Curriculum," especially pages 344–352. Conclusions: A capstone of applying technology in the classroom and how to blend technology with the curriculum other modes of teaching.

Curriculum Recommendations Integrating technology in learning environments and computer-aided instruction.

Project Recommendations Develop a school technology staff development plan, and require a student to download the Level of Technology Integration Self-Report (LoTi) and administer to classmates.

Function I

Monitor and evaluate the impact of the instructional program.

References

1. Wong, K., & Nicotera, A. (2007). *Successful schools and educational accountability*. Boston: Pearson. Conclusions: Addresses the effects of standards and the accountability movement on teachers and school leaders as well as the impact on learning.
2. Yeh, S. (2006). Can rapid assessment moderate the consequences of high-stakes testing? *Education and Urban Society*, 39(1), 91–112. Conclusions: This study suggests how rapid assessment can foster balanced instruction and positive use of test results for improved teaching and learning.

Curriculum Recommendations Instructional management, program evaluation, and curriculum development.

Project Recommendations Ask the students to monitor a curriculum area of their choice and observe the outcomes of student interest in the subject (i.e., art, projects and portfolios. Does student interest reach beyond traditional learning outcomes?)

Standard 3

An education leader promotes the success of every student by ensuring management of the organization, operation, and resources for a safe, efficient, and effective learning environment.

Function A

Monitor and evaluate the management and operational systems.

References

1. Rodriquez, G., & Rolle, A. (2007). *To what ends and by what means? The social justice implications of contemporary school finance theory and policy.* New York: Routledge. Conclusions: A thorough look at the ethical use of funding to help assure equality for all students.
2. Bingham, W., & Jones, T. (2008). School district and financial operations. In J. Vornberg (Ed.). *Texas public school organization and administration.* Dubuque, IA: Kendall Hunt Publishers, 395–411. Conclusions: The big picture of school district operations and budgeting planning and evaluation.
3. Creighton, T. (2006). *The educators guide for using data to improve decision making.* Thousand Oaks, CA: Corwin Press. Conclusions: Improve instructional leadership through proven, easy-to-understand strategies for data-based decision making.
4. Ulrich, D., Zenger, J., & Smallwood, J. (1999). *Results-based leadership: How leaders build the business and improve the bottom line.* Boston: Harvard Press. Conclusions: Improve the teaching and learning culture and what leaders must know about how humans learn.
5. Hoyle, J., English, F., & Steffy, B. (1998). *Skills for successful 21st century school leaders.* Lanham, MD: Rowman & Littlefield Education, pages 53–60. Conclusions: This is a very readable account of how to conduct student centered operational management in schools and school districts.

Curriculum Recommendations Courses in school business management, principalship, superintendency, or economics of school management.

Project Recommendations Require each student to review their school or school district budgets and justify the allocation and expenditure of funds based on district mission for student learning.

Function B

Obtain, allocate, align, and efficiently utilize human, fiscal, and technological resources.

References

1. Guthrie, J., Springer, M., Rolle, R., & Houch, E. A. (2007). *Modern educational finance and policy.* Boston: Allyn & Bacon. Conclusions: A top rated book on school finance and the economic applications to collection and distribution of funds for schools.

2. Rolle, A. (2004). *Peabody journal of education: Special issue on K-12 education finance—New directions for future research.* 79(3). Mahwah, N.J.: Lawrence Erlbaum. Conclusions: The author leads the reader into new perspectives on research about how to link fiscal knowledge to school operations.
3. Hoyle, J., Bjork, L., Collier, V., & Glass, T. (2005). *The superintendent as CEO: Standards-based performance.* Thousand Oaks, Calif.: Corwin Press. Conclusions: This book and chapter 5 is closely aligned with NCATE and the AASA national standards.
4. Guthrie, J., & Schuermann, P. (2010) *Successful school leadership: Planning, politics, performance, and power.* Boston: Allyn & Bacon, pages 59–61 and 263–291. Conclusions: chapter 3 is an excellent account of strategic planning and goal setting and chapter 11 is a very thorough account of data-based decision making to guide programs, personnel, and resource allocation decisions.

Curriculum Recommendations Courses in superintendency, educational policy, and operational systems in education, business, or public finance.

Project Recommendations Ask each student to bring to class and discuss the school district three- to five-year plan that includes the vision/mission statement, operational goals, assessment processes, personnel responsibilities, and budget allocations.

Function C

Promote and protect the welfare and safety of students and staff.

References

1. Beaudoin, M., & Taylor, M. (2009). *Responding to the culture of bullying and disrespect.* Thousand Oaks, Calif.: Corwin Press. Conclusions: New ideas on strategies to eliminate bullying and intimidation of students.
2. Cunningham, B., & Cordeiro. (2000). *Educational administration: A problem based approach.* Boston: Allyn Bacon, see chapter 9, "Pupil personnel services," and pages 267–271 for specific material. Conclusions: An excellent overview of the legal and caring side of keeping schools a safe place to work and learn.
3. Hoyle, J., English, F., & Steffy, B. (1998). *Skills for successful 21st century school leaders.* Lanham, Md.: Rowman & Littlefield Education, 4–12. Conclusions: Advice on how to cultivate, captivate and celebrate a safe, threat-free environment for all students and staff. Also, find several teacher and student self-report climate assessment questionnaires.

Curriculum Recommendations Classroom management, principalship, personnel evaluation, program evaluation, and school law.

Project Recommendations Assign one of the readings and ask for an oral report from at least two students and then create a role-playing situation on bullying a boy or girl at the middle school level.

Function D

Develop the capacity for distributed leadership.

References

1. Spillane, J. (2007). *Distributive leadership in practice.* New York: Teachers College Press. Conclusions: An excellent account of how distributive leadership works and its unique qualities compared to leadership models.
2. Hoyle, J. (2002). *Leadership and the force of love: Six steps to motivating with love.* Thousand Oaks, Calif.: Corwin Press, 48–59 and 61–68.
3. Wilmore, E. (2002b). *The principalship: Applying the new educational leadership constituent council (ELLC) standards.* Thousand Oaks, Calif.: Corwin Press, 19–30 and 66–78. Conclusions: Very relevant to this function and skill and easy to follow.

Curriculum Recommendations Courses in leadership/organizational theory, human relations, futurism and global change, superintendency, and prinicipalship.

Project Recommendations Create a role-playing situation where students portray school principals with two extreme leadership styles striving for higher student performance on a state-wide high stake test. Principal one uses a dictatorial, no excuses leadership style while principal two uses a distributive leadership style.

Function E

Ensure teacher and organizational time is focused to support quality instruction and student learning.

References

1. Goodlad, J. (1984) *A place called school: Prospects for the future.* New York: McGraw-Hill, 93–129. Conclusions: This landmark book set the stage for the value of time on task for student learning.
2. Bloom, B. (1982). *All our children's learning.* New York: McGraw-Hill. Conclusions: A classic text on the value of varying time on task for each student to help him or her master the material.

3. Berliner, D. (1988). Simple views of effective teaching and simple theory of classroom instruction. In D. Berliner & B. Rosenshine (Eds.) *Talks to teachers*, 93–110. New York: Random House. Conclusions: Berliner found that almost every study examining time on task and learning has a significant relationship between time spent on content and student learning.
4. Hoyle, J., English, F., & Steffy, B. (1998). *Skills for successful 21st century school leaders*. Lanham, Md.: Rowman & Littlefield Education, 85–103. Conclusions: A good overview of the power of motivated students with enough time-on-task and their higher achievement levels.

Curriculum Recommendations Course in instructional management, psychology of learning or classroom supervision.

Project Recommendations Create four focus groups and assign each group one the four readings. Ask each team to report on their reading and provide examples of learning time management in their school settings.

Standard 4

An education leader promotes the success of every student by collaborating with faculty and community members, responding to diverse community interests and needs and mobilizing community resources.

Function A

Collect and analyze data and information pertinent to the educational environment.

References

1. Guthrie, J., & Schuermann, P. (2010). *Successful school leadership*. Boston: Allyn & Bacon, 233–263 and 263–297. Conclusions: An account of what school leaders must do to apply data to decisions.
2. Hoyle, J., Bjork, L., Collier, V., & Glass, T. (2005) *The superintendent as CEO: Standards-based performance*. Thousand Oaks: Calif.: Corwin, 59–78, 109–126, and 127–157. Conclusions: chapters 4, 6, and 7 are excellent accounts of the community, diverse learners, and using data to inform teaching and improve student achievement.

Curriculum Recommendations Community relations, sociology of communities, urban education, superintendency, program evaluation, and the prinicipalship.

Project Recommendations Require students to write a three-page paper that includes perception of their student population, their current achievement levels in the basic subjects, and types of interventions underway to improve student learning, school attendance, and behavior.

Function B

Promote understanding, appreciation, and use of the community's diverse cultural, social, and intellectual resources.

References

1. Rothstein, R. (2004). *Class and school. Using social, economic, and educational reform to close the black-white gap.* New York: Teachers College Press. Conclusions: This is a comprehensive look at the issues of diversity in terms of race, closing the achievement gaps, and understanding cultural and social dynamics.
2. Green, R. (2010). *The four dimensions of principal leadership.* Boston: Allyn & Bacon (Pearson), see chapter 4 which also relates to standards two and three. Conclusions: A very compact well-written book that covers the issues of community, culture, interactions of people, and diverse needs of students.

Curriculum Recommendations Multicultural education, social foundations, urban education, curriculum for diversity, and the principalship.

Project Recommendations Assign each student a chapter or chapter from each of the two empirical references, divide class into groups of four and apply the nominal group technique. After approximately one hour, each group will present their three solutions to helping all students in diverse settings become prepared for successful lives and careers.

Function C

Build and sustain positive relationships with families and caregivers.

References

1. Hoyle, J., Bjork, L., Collier, V., & Glass, T. (2005). *The superintendent as CEO: Standards based performance.* Thousand Oaks, Calif.: Corwin Press. See chapter 4, "Community and community relations." Conclusions: This chapter is very comprehensive on each cultural and family issue of Standard 4 and Function C.
2. Rodriquez, G., & Fabionar, J. (2010). The impact of poverty on students and schools: Exploring the social justice leadership implications. In C. Marshall & M. Oliva (Eds.) *Leadership for social justice.*

Boston: Allyn & Bacon. Conclusions: chapter 4 is an excellent account of the systemic impact of poverty on school communities and families.

3. Green, R. (2010) *The four dimensions of principal leadership.* Boston: Allyn & Bacon (Pearson). Chapter 4, "The social interaction in schools." Conclusions: A well-written account on the issues of community involvement and leadership.

Curriculum Recommendations Social foundations, special populations in education, multicultural education, urban education, principalship, and superintendency.

Project Recommendations Assign each student to review his or her district demographic predictions for the next five years and write a paper on ways in which the community and family structures may change.

Function D

Build and sustain productive relationships with community partners.

References

1. Hoyle, J., Bjork, L., Collier, V., & Glass, T. (2005). *The superintendent as CEO: Standards-based performance.* Thousand Oaks, Calif.: Corwin Press. See chapter 4, "Community and community relations." Conclusions: This chapter is very comprehensive on each cultural and family issue of Standard 4 and Function C.
2. Rodriquez, G., & Fabionar, J. (2010). The impact of poverty on students and schools: Exploring the social justice leadership implications. In C. Marshall & M. Oliva (Eds.) *Leadership for social justice.* Boston: Allyn & Bacon. Conclusions: chapter 4 is an excellent account of the systemic impact of poverty on school communities and families.
3. Green, R. (2010) *The four dimensions of principal leadership.* Boston: Allyn & Bacon (Pearson). Chapter 4, "The social interaction in schools." Conclusions: A well-written account on the issues of community involvement and leadership.

Curriculum Recommendations Social foundations, special populations in education, multicultural education, urban education, principalship, and superintendency.

Project Recommendations Assign each student to review his or her district demographic predictions for the next five years and write a paper on ways in which the community and family structures may change.

Standard 5

An education leader promotes the success of every student by acting with integrity, fairness, and in an ethical manner.

Function A

Ensure a system of accountability for every student's academic and social success.

References

1. Badgett, J., & Christmann, E. (2009b). *Designing middle and high school instruction and assessment*. Thousand Oaks, Calif.: Corwin Press. Conclusions: This is the best book on a step-by-step approach to student assessment at the middle and secondary school levels. Following this book will help ensure that the accountability system will work for students.
2. Strike, K. (2007). *Ethical leadership in schools*. Thousand Oaks, Calif.: Corwin Press. Conclusions: An excellent book that teaches aspiring principals the concepts that inform ethical choices as a school leader. The book guides leaders through the process of making multiple ethical decisions.
3. Jazzar, M., & Algozzine, B. (2007). *Keys to successful 21st century educational leadership*. Boston: Pearson. See chapter 9, "Legal and moral leadership: Doing the right thing" Conclusions: The chapter begins with a case study and challenges the reader to reflect on five excellent questions about ethical decision making.
4. Hoyle, J., Bjork, L., Collier, V., & Glass, T. (2005). *The superintendent as CEO: Standards-based performance*. Thousand Oaks, Calif.: Corwin Press. See chapter 9, "Values and ethics." Conclusions: The chapter begins with superintendent Ron Jones facing a very difficult moral dilemma involving religious belief systems. The chapter covers each of key skills, functions, and theoretical frameworks of ethics for school leaders.

Curriculum Recommendations Superintendency, principalship, school law, and ethics in educational leadership, program evaluation and measurement and assessment.

Project Recommendations Require class to read the case studies in references 3 and 4, and assign students to participate in role-playing about the ethical issues around leadership and student success.

Function B

Model principles of self-awareness, reflective practice, transparency, and ethical behavior.

References

1. Cunningham, W., & Cordeiro, P. (2003). *Educational leadership. A problem-based approach.* Boston: Allyn & Bacon, 185–202. Conclusions: An excellent roadmap for building an ethical school with an ethic of caring.
2. Slattery, P., & Rapp, D. (2003). *Ethics and the foundations of education.* Boston: Pearson. Conclusions: Explores ethical issues in schools and society from the vantage point of critical theory and the democratic community. The book includes stories and cases to explore.

Curriculum Recommendations Foundations of educations, ethics in leadership, organizational theory, and leadership in education, superintendency, and principalship.

Project Recommendations Ask students to write a three-page paper applying concepts of social justice to ethical leadership by a school principal. Ask for volunteers to present their paper to the group.

Function C

Safeguard the values of democracy, equity, and diversity.

References

1. Strike, K. (2007). *Ethical leadership in schools.* Thousand Oaks, Calif.: Corwin Press, 43–110. Conclusions: The chapters include excellent material on intellectual liberty, religious freedom, intellectual community, equal opportunity, multicultural community, democracy, community and accountability. The best, most readable material for Function C.
2. Torres, M. (2004). Best interests of students left behind? Exploring the ethical and legal dimensions of United States involvement in public school improvement. *Journal of Educational Administration,* 42(2), 249–269. Conclusions: A thorough look at the legal and ethical issues of all students in danger of being left behind.

Curriculum Recommendations Principalship, superintendency, school law, and ethical foundations (in education, philosophy, or sociology).

Project Recommendations After reading the three chapters by Strike, ask the students to provide written and oral examples of their ethical leadership in promoting democracy, equity, and celebrating diversity.

Function D

Consider and evaluate the potential moral and legal consequences of decision making.

References

1. Hoy, W., & Tarter, J. (1995). *Administrators solving the problems of practice: Decision making, concepts, cases, and consequences.* Boston: Allyn & Bacon, 117–166. Conclusions: A thorough look at decision-making models in educational leadership and the implications about ethical decisions.
2. Wilmore, E. (2002a). *Principal leadership.* Thousand Oaks, Calif.: Corwin Press, 80–91. Conclusions: A brief and direct link to the standard of ethics in school leadership.
3. Hoyle, J. (2009). The educational leader: Diplomat and communicator for all students. In P. Houston, P. Blankenship, and R. Cole (Eds.). *Leaders as communicators and diplomats.* Thousand Oaks, Calif.: Corwin Press. See chapter 3. Conclusions: This collection of readings is excellent in leading graduate students to think about the spiritual, moral, and diplomatic dimensions of leadership in schools.

Curriculum Recommendations Principalship, ethics in leadership, and organizational theory and leadership in schools.

Project Recommendations Read Hoyle's chapter in *Leaders as communicators and Diplomats.* Organize class into pro and con debate teams and ask them to debate the ethics of the principal allowing migrant students to miss school and keep them on the class roles. That is, should school leaders break district policy to help some students succeed?

Function E

Promote social justice and ensure that individual student needs inform all aspects of schooling.

References

1. Scheurich, J., & Skrla, L. (2003). *Leadership for equity and excellence.* Thousand Oaks, Calif.: Corwin Press. Conclusions: Helps school leaders and teachers develop strategies for student equity, audits, and deep caring for each learner.
2. Harris, S. (2006). *Best practices of award winning secondary school principals.* Thousand Oaks, Calif.: Corwin Press. Conclusions: Over 100 successful strategies for secondary principals to promote and insure the individual learning needs of students.
3. Sergiovanni, T. (2006). *Rethinking leadership: A collection of articles.* Thousand Oaks, Calif.: Corwin Press. Conclusions: Rethinking the craft of moral leadership to help all students and teachers build productive learning communities.

4. Hoyle, J., & Crenshaw, H. (1996). *Interpersonal sensitivity*. Larchmont, N.Y.: Eye on Education. See student and staff self-report "Sensitivity Scales." Conclusions: Written to explore the power of interpersonal sensitivity in leading students and staff to greater respect for self and others in order to create successful learning communities. See the self-report questionnaires to assess the interpersonal skills of principals and teachers.

Curriculum Recommendations Principalship, supervision of instruction, human relations in schools, and motivation in education.

Projects Recommendations Select or create a case study about a school with wide gaps in student achievement. Ask each student to decide what three or four factors created the achievement gap. Next organize class into three or four focus groups and ask them to decide what changes they would make to help promote and insure that the gap will be narrowed.

Standard 6

An education leader promotes the success of every student by understanding, responding to, and influencing the political, social, economic, legal, and cultural context.

Function A

Advocate for children, families, and caregivers.

References

1. Torres, M., & Chen, Y. (2006). Assessing Columbine's impact on students' fourth amendment case outcomes: Implications for administrative discretion and decision making. *NASSP Bulletin*, 90(3), 185–206. Conclusions: An excellent article on administrative discretion and decision making in crisis situations.
2. Goddard, R. (2003). Relational networks, social trust, and norms. A social capital perspective on students' chances of academic success. *Educational Evaluation and Policy Analysis*, 62(1), 59–74. Conclusions: A student self-report of the school's level of trust and support for their academic and social success.
3. Spring, J. (2002). *American education* (10th ed.). Boston: McGraw-Hill. See chapter 1, "The purpose of schooling," chapter 4, "Equality of opportunity and social class," and chapter 9, "Power and control at the state and national levels: Accountability, high stakes testing, school violence, and reading and math wars, and private foundations." Conclusions: An excellent introduction to the historical, political, social,

and legal foundations of education and to the profession of teaching and administration.

4. Dunklee, D., & Shoop, R. (2001). *The principal's quick reference guide to school law: Reducing liability, litigation, and other potential legal tangles.* Thousand Oaks, Calif.: Corwin Press. Conclusions: A good source for busy principals to help them avoid legal pitfalls.
5. Rothstein, R. (2004). *Class and schools.* New York: Teachers College Press. Conclusions: A good look at how social class shapes learning outcomes and learning styles. Rothstein calls for a transformation of social and labor policy along with other reforms.
6. Peterson, K., & Deal, T. (2002). *Shaping school culture field book.* San Francisco: Jossey Bass. Conclusions: An excellent field book with examples on how to explore the dimensions of culture and strategies to shape the culture so that the climate is positive for all students and faculty.

Curriculum Recommendations Principalship, school law, foundations of educational administration, organizational theory, and program evaluation (emphasis on student assessment data).

Project Recommendations Require students to contact local child welfare services and local law enforcement officials about families in need and what schools can do to work with various agencies to help students in troubled situations.

Function B

Act to influence local, state, district, and national decisions affecting student learning.

References

1. Goddard, R., & LoGerfo, L. (2007). Measuring emergent organizational properties: A comparison of the predictive validity and intergroup variability of self vs group referent perceptions. *Educational and Psychological Measurement,* 65(5), 845–858. Conclusions: A good model for assessing the importance of organizational dimensions.
2. Rebore, R., & Walmsley, A. (2007). *An evidence based approach to the practice of educational leadership.* Boston: Pearson, 156–183. Conclusions: A good overview of the critical technical core elements (i.e., assessing the curriculum, disaggregating the data, instructional strategies, administrator's role, and the evaluation cycle).
3. Razik, T., & Swanson, A. (2010). *Fundamental concepts of educational leadership and management.* Boston: Allyn & Bacon, 245–277 and 278–306. Conclusions: These chapters provide an excellent overview

of the creation and implementation of educational policy at the national, state, and local levels. Also, the reader will find helpful information about decision making and policy at the district and school levels.

4. Vornberg, J. (2008). Systematic approach to educational accountability: Standards, programs, and procedures in Texas. In J. Vornberg (Ed.) *Texas public school organization and administration: 2008,* 113–42. Dubuque, Iowa: Kendall Hunt Publishers. Conclusions: An excellent account of how state accountability systems affect student learning, teaching, and assessment.

Curriculum Recommendations Program evaluation, tests and measurement, educational politics, and policy.

Project Recommendations Assign class member to read either of the recommended readings and report on the relationships to local policy and impact on students to their current roles in schools.

Function C

Analyze and anticipate emerging trends and initiatives in order to adapt leadership strategies.

References

1. Hoyle, J. (2007c). *Leadership and futuring: Making visions happen.* Thousand Oaks, Calif.: Corwin Press, 75–98. Conclusions: See the visionary step-by-step plan underway in Huntsville, Texas, as a result of anticipating emerging trends and community visioning to help assure every child succeeds in the future.
2. Cornish, E. (2004). *Futuring: The exploration of the future.* Bethesda, Md.: World Future Society, 22–36. Conclusions: A wonderful source for helping school leaders anticipate the future by analyzing trends and a wide range of national and world initiatives.
3. Brubaker, D. (2006) *The charismatic leader.* Thousand Oaks, Calif.: Corwin Press. Conclusions: Essential skills that promote effective exchange of information and better relationships to help anticipate trends and initiatives to guide changes in leadership styles and processes.

Curriculum Recommendations Futurism and global change, change theory, and leadership for social justice.

Project Recommendations Organize class into groups of six members and ask them to move into the future fifteen years. Inform them that on this day, fifteen years in the future, each group has won the national prize for the most student-centered, high-performing school district in the United States. Create a leader for each group (e.g., ask who in the group has the smallest pet) thus, we have a spokesperson. Next ask each group to identify three to four steps they took fifteen years earlier to become the best district in the United States. Ask each team to report their findings to the class via a mock international news conference.

Summary

We recommend that faculty use this guide to assure that each student will master the content provided in the each of the six standards and related functions. The students will be well grounded in the minimum accepted knowledge base that will serve them well as practitioners or beginning doctoral students. In addition, the students should pass the state examinations for licensure. We have included carefully selected empirical readings and classroom simulation or discussion projects and activities.

Also, find suggested curricula linked to each function in educational administration, curriculum, educational psychology, and measurement for the master's degree plan. It has been our experience that degree program revision can create considerable confusion and frustration among faculty when they lack some structure. The information found in this step should ease the confusion and help program planners create a solid degree for future school principals. We suggest that this step be distributed to each faculty member before discussing program or degree revisions.

DOCTORAL DEGREE: RECOMMENDED READINGS AND PROJECTS

After two professors assess the quality of beginning doctoral students' responses to each of the six questions, the following readings and projects are offered to assist faculty in advising students who were marginal on their responses. We repeat each question and suggest appropriate readings and independent projects that will help assure that the student is ready to compete with classmates who graded excellent or good on the diagnostic essay exam.

Question 1

Discuss four major crises in U.S. education and provide possible solutions.

Readings

1. Furman, S., & Lazerson, M. (Eds.). (2005). *The public schools.* Philadelphia: University of Pennsylvania Press. See chapters 2, 3, and 6. Conclusions: A scholarly overview of crises facing public schools as instruments of democracy.
2. Rothstein, R. (2004). *Class and schools.* New York: Teachers College Press. Conclusions: A persuasive analysis of how social class shapes learning outcomes and forces us to rethink how to educate all children.
3. Guthrie, J., & Schuermann, P. (2010). *Successful school leadership.* Boston: Allyn & Bacon. See chapters 1 and 2. Conclusions: A very good look at key historical forces of change and their impact on the organization and strategic leadership in schools.

Project Recommendations

Assign the student selected readings and conduct an oral exam of question 1.

Question 2

Identify and discuss research underway to discover links between principal and superintendent leadership responsibilities and student academic performance (5–8 pages).

Readings

1. Waters, J. T., & Marzano, R. (2006). *School district leadership that works: The effect of superintendent leadership on student achievement.* Denver: Mid-continent Research for Education and Learning.
2. Marzano, R., Waters, T., & McNulty, B. (2005). *School leadership that works: From research to results.* Alexandria, Va.: Association for Supervision and Curriculum Development.
3. Leithwood, K., & Levin, B (2005). Assessing leadership effects on student learning. In W. Hoy & C. Miskel (Eds.). *Contemporary issues in educational policy and school outcomes,* 53–76. Greenwich, Conn.: Information Age.

Project Recommendations

Ask the student to draw on the latest findings by Waters and Marzano and the current work by Leithwood that investigates the links between administrator leadership behaviors and student academic success.

Question 3

Identify the current inequities in public and private school education and suggest solutions.

Readings

1. Ramirez, D., & Severn, L. (2006). Gap or Gaps: Challenging the singular definition of the achievement gap. *Education and Urban Society,* 39(1), 113–28.
2. Quigney, T. (2008). The reauthorization of the No Child Left Behind act: Recommended practices regarding teaching students with disabilities. *Planning and Changing,* 39(3&4), 146–158.
3. Lachmann, L. M., & Taylor, L. (1995). *Schools for all: Educating children in a diverse society.* Albany: Delmar Publishers, 1–65.

Project Recommendations

Ask student to review the suggested readings and conduct an oral exam based on question 3.

Question 4

Explain the manner in which schools are financed and suggest ways to improve the current system.

Readings

1. Guthrie, J., Springer, M., Rolle, R., & Houch, E. A. (2007). *Modern educational finance and policy.* Boston: Allyn & Bacon.
2. Baker, B. (2009). Within-district resource allocation and the marginal costs of providing equal opportunity: Evidence from Texas and Ohio. *Education policy analysis archives,* 17(3), 1–28.
3. Byrd, J., & Drews, C. (2008). The relationship between resource allocation and student achievement. *School Leadership Review,* 3(2), 35–65.

Project Recommendations

Ask student to review portions of the suggested readings and conduct oral exam on basic school finance and its applications to system improvements.

Question 5

What education policy would you like to initiate that could lead to a major reform in public education?

Readings

1. Corcoran, T., & Goertz, M. (2005). The governance of public education. In S. Furman and M. Lazerson (Eds.) *The public schools*, 25–57. Philadelphia: The Annenberg Foundation.
2. Hoyle, J., Bjork, L., Collier, V., & Glass, T. (2005). *The superintendent as CEO; Standards-based performance.* Thousand Oaks, Calif.: Corwin Press, 35–58.

Project Recommendations

Review the two readings and ask the student to provide an oral response to question 5.

Question 6

What is the value of organizational theory to the practical operation of schools and school districts?

Readings

1. Cunningham, W., & Cordeiro, P. (2006). *Educational leadership* (3rd ed.). Boston: Pearson, 1–28 and 153–189.
2. Hoy, W., & Miskel, C. (2008). *Educational administration: Theory, research, and practice.* Boston: McGraw-Hill, 1–39.

Project Recommendations

Ask student to review the two readings and ask for the definition, meaning and application to theory to daily practice in schools.

Summary

After students have successfully responded to all or part of the questions, they should be better prepared to begin classes with the cohort or classmates. We find that this process also has been helpful at qualifying examination time after the student has completed all course work. Adding new questions or adapting these six to your programs can enhance the comprehensive examination.

5

Step Four

Creating and Maintaining Effective Student Advisory Committees

Another facet of leadership programming that captures sparse attention but nonetheless plays a critical role is the role of student advisory committees at both the master's and doctoral levels. In most programs, students are required to have committees who are responsible for overseeing and monitoring the intellectual and practice-based development of students. In most cases, the committees' level of involvement is sporadic and irregular.

Ordinarily, committees are assigned at the point when students enter the program. In some cases, the committees' only charge is to dispense and evaluate questions for a comprehensive examination. We argue that committees need to assume a larger stake in the process. It is not easy for professors to devote limited time to committee meetings in most graduate programs in educational leadership. In research-intensive universities, time constraints hinder the amount of time and energy that professors can devote to the practical dimensions of leadership that are not always purely scholarly nor academic in nature.

Among the more time-consuming tasks for professors is advising new students about the curriculum, degree plans, composition of the graduate faculty committee, and the examination processes. The most time-consuming scholarly activity for the committee chair is providing oversight of the doctoral dissertation topic and the research procedures. This responsibility for faculty is perhaps the most stressful of many tasks for the committee chair who guides the student through comprehensive examinations, proposal creation, and dissertation advisement, and final defense.

The stress for faculty grows when other members of the student's committee may not find time to read the proposal prior to the committee meeting but then during the meeting question the relevance or quality of the research topic and proposal. In addition, after a student's proposal is approved by the committee and graduate school, the burden of supervision of the study falls on the committee chair. Other committee members may have received individuals chapters of the study, but due to other demands fail to read them until the final defense is scheduled.

The student and committee chair assume that the document is ready to defend since no feedback was received from the other committee members. It is not uncommon for a committee member to approach the committee chair one day or two hours before the defense and raise serious objections to the document. The student or the committee chair should never face this kind of pressure due to poor communication among the committee. This often troubling issue of dissertation oversight will be presented in greater detail later in this chapter.

In this step, we offer our best advice on procedures to improve the operations of graduate committees to help guide graduate students through the pressure-filled maze leading to licensure and graduation. We have drawn on numerous documents detailing the roles of graduate committees.

We thank our colleagues at the following institutions: The University of Southern Mississippi developed by professors Thelma Robertson and Rose McNeese; George Washington University; California Lutheran University; Seton Hall University; Lamar University; Alabama State University; and Texas A&M University. These documents together added insight into the important role of graduate committees guiding students through their degrees and the dissertation process.

In today's context where professors are largely rewarded for articles and books published, graduate faculty often lose sight of their vital roles serving as members of graduate committees. Our literature reviews and personal observations reveal inconsistent patterns of graduate committee members' participation among leadership programs nationwide and in Canada. We suggest ways to maximize faculty talent serving on student advisory committees to enrich students' graduate academic and field experiences and ways to improve the effectiveness of graduate advisory committees to help ensure higher quality classroom performance, guide students to higher performance final or qualifying examination, and improve the quality of theses or dissertations.

MAXIMIZING THE UTILIZATION OF APPLIED PERSONNEL

First and foremost, clinical faculty with a record of success in leading schools for all children must be utilized more effectively on graduate committees by utilizing their knowledge to tighten the link between theory and practice. More times than not, clinical faculty are assigned to teach courses with a strong applied focus such as plant management, the principalship, and the superintendency. The invaluable insight and perspectives clinical faculty provide are a necessary component of any leadership program. However, the responsibilities of clinical faculty are often too vague and ill defined.

In other words, programs give little consideration to ways in which clinical faculty and school leaders in the field can add a valuable element to the development of leaders. Some programs do not expect clinical or adjunct faculty to attend faculty meetings and other task force sessions to update degree requirements and research expectations of faculty and students. Thus, the full-time faculty, who feel that they do the real work of the department in program development, student advisement, and service assignments on campus, often consider the adjunct and clinical faculty as outsiders coming in to teach a class but not serving on students' committees.

We strongly suggest students' graduate committees need both university scholars and clinical faculty to guide students in both the theoretical and applied components of leadership. A balance between the full-time and clinical faculty on each committee may help reduce the growing skepticism of leadership programming in general and its capacity to prepare leaders for the challenges of modern public education (Levine 2005; Elmore 2007; Murphy 2007). Take for instance a study by Orr, Berg, Shore, and Meier (2008) that found principals were unable to effectively lead and facilitate collective action around student performance.

The following describes experiences of school leaders of four low performing middle schools in the New York City area:

> Little or no capacity for collective problem solving, growth, and development existed in the schools generally, even in noninstructional areas. For example, one school, in developing its comprehensive education plans, collected instructional improvement ideas from each instructional coach and assistant principal and combined them with the test data results; there was no discussion or collective review about performance, target goals, and strategies and little implementation follow-up the next year to monitor use of the strategies and their effects on achievement.
>
> Finally, even when groups of teachers and school leaders were trained in a new intervention or instructional support, implementation was left to each individual, with little collective discussion, turnkey training with other staff, or follow-through on how to integrate new interventions with other strategies (684–685).

This illustration happens with greater frequency in school systems than one might think. Of primary concern is that principals who successfully complete programs even in the most prestigious programs suffer skill deficits. In the preceding case, the principals were unable to draw upon sources of knowledge acquired in the classroom or elsewhere to lead the implementation of the ambitious reform in a coherent and thoughtful way. We feel that by more fully tapping into the talents and insight of applied experts serving on student committees, school leaders will be better equipped to face the challenges of school change and improvement.

HONORING KNOWLEDGE OF PRACTICE AS A LEGITIMATE SPHERE OF KNOWLEDGE

Educational leadership programs must be inclusive of diverse knowledge bases, namely the intellectual and applied contributions of clinical faculty and leaders in the field. Davidson (as cited in Trowler 1998) notes that education as a discipline differs considerably from the more hierarchically developed knowledge found in the natural sciences, computer science, and even language.

Comparing "linear" with "nonlinear" disciplines, Davidson suggests that education lacks the "inherently modular structure" (Trowler 1998, 57) found in linear forms of disciplines. Knowledge in linear disciplines is transmitted in "packets" and sequenced in a "pyramid" like process. Education, as Davidson suggests, deals less with concrete theory and law and relies extensively upon accumulated experience and knowledge that is far less centralized and far more contested.

While knowledge of teaching and learning has advanced over the years, education as a discipline remains fragmented and divided. The causes of this are complex. Some of it is purely epistemological, some of it political, some cultural. Whatever the case may be, our knowledge of school leadership remains rather primitive. Bjork and Ginsberg (1995) express the following concerning educational administration as a discipline:

> First, departments of educational administration should stop pretending they are true preparadigm fields. As has been discussed, educational administration has traditionally tried to act like these mature disciplines but, for a number of reasons, cannot and will not achieve parity in terms of academic prestige (30).

Bjork and Ginsberg later suggest the following:

> A key is for the field to attempt to capture useful components of mature paradigm fields that are achievable. This goal would be directed toward ensuring that future faculty in the educational administration community would undergo similar training and initiation, as exemplars, share commitment to

> a set of beliefs, values, and examples that reflect fundamental changes in the field. Obviously, a willingness to derive new approaches to training from like disciplines (e.g., other professional schools) is needed (31).

To advance a discipline, a broader array of information must be sought. As with most academic institutions, a primary cornerstone is the constant pursuit of a marketplace of ideas and respect for multiple and competing viewpoints. It is therefore vital that a student's graduate committee represent competing viewpoints about successful leadership in schools.

At times however, academic disciplines can create elite cultures that reject categories of information that are deemed less important or lack scientific grounding. For example, in a prior study by Hoyle and Torres (2008) examining student perceptions of leadership program preparation for practice, one student from a highly ranked private university program remarked "students were not required to take a course in organizational behavior or theory and were exposed to little about administration" (229). This alarming statement is representative of other students experiencing preparation programs missing a common knowledge core basic to preparing future school leaders.

For programs to remain relevant and committed to children achieving, it is crucial for programs to capitalize on knowledge from the field. Scholars who study organizations consistently acknowledge the complexity of schools and the need to carefully consider countless internal and external dimensions. As Weick (1995) believes, a critical aspect often overlooked when organizational settings such as schools are investigated is the cognitive framework used to interpret events.

According to Weick (1995), making sense or meaning of problems or issues demands an active and engaged process aimed toward understanding, interpreting, explaining, reflecting, reconciling, deliberating, connecting, and being aware of stimuli. It is far from an idle process of interpretation, which fails to utilize stimuli to "invent" and construct meaning.

When organizational "sense-making" is attempted, it often falls well short of a fully comprehensive and objective analysis. Political and rhetorical manipulation renders outcomes ambiguous and distorted. In genuine sense-making, a greater effort is made to piece together information so that it supports an active investigation of outcomes (e.g., both unforeseen and uncertain) from multiple perspectives. Be that as it may, scarce research exists that comprehensively addresses the use of field knowledge through committees to generate understanding of field-based issues.

Weick (1995) further maintains that organizations rely on a false sense of what is appropriate to solve a problem rather than a concerted effort to explore sources of the problem. Then again, never before have schools faced such a complex set of social, cultural, and economic circumstances. In sum, committees must engender a spirit of community, respect, and collective responsibility in the development of students' intellectual capacity and skills of practice.

FORGING EFFECTIVE AND LASTING STUDENT SUPPORT STRUCTURES

In addition to coursework, students will need additional types of support and consultation from members of the faculty and the field. Whether it is through academic support, scholarly collaboration, or professional support, the makeup and design of student advisory committees must serve the best interests of students.

To achieve an effective support structure for students, the design of the committee must reflect the mission of the program. Committees, which may include nontraditional participants such as nonfaculty leaders in the field, community leaders, and other influential constituencies, should be equally contributing members to the development of school leaders. We recommend as well that students who complete the program have access to the program support structure indefinitely and that committee members commit to this lifelong support.

Reinventing student advisory committees will demand that participants be open to new ways of operating and realize that leadership encompasses many aspects not covered in textbooks and lectures. Similar to the "useful strategic knowledge" proposed by Leithwood and Steinbach (1992), aspects would reflect "explicit strategies and heuristics in our research with expertise, as well as the (usually) tacit knowledge required for its actual use in real-life administrative contexts" (322).

It will entail new relationships, new ways of communicating, nontraditional ways of supporting student learning and practice, and greater solidarity between the university and the field. Such a change will not come easy. Grogan and Andrews (2002) describe the challenges to adopting innovative administrative structures:

> Collegiality is part of the rhetoric, but individual achievement receives the highest rewards and status. Professors still "own" courses. Although university instructors have much more autonomy than the average school teacher, the system of higher education reinforces the same isolation as we have traditionally seen in schools. We, in the academy, need to take seriously the research on the value of teaming and building partnerships. If university raises and bonuses followed evidence of cooperation among faculty members, and if foundations were to make it a priority to fund collaborative projects between districts and universities, the incentives would reinforce the beliefs (251).

Departing from routines that have long been in place will require a consideration of program culture, attitudes, values, and skills.

Other disciplines have pursued novel ways to enrich the learning experience of their graduates that is far removed from the status quo. A promising collaboration titled the Clinical Scientist Associate (CSA) program formed between the University of Pittsburgh School of Pharmacy and the University of Pittsburgh School of Medicine. In the University School of Pharmacy both units agreed a partnership would result in outcomes that would be mutually beneficial.

Of growing concern to the school of pharmacy was that an overemphasis on developing researchers and scientists might overshadow the importance of clinical experiences, which would run counter to the current demands of the industry. In view of the increasingly clinical nature of research practices within the pharmaceutical industry, it was difficult for the school of pharmacy to conceive doctoral education absent the clinical strand that stressed practical skills.

By integrating clinical work, the partnership is able to extend a level of financial support to full time doctoral students in the program that is nearly equivalent of an average part-time pharmacist salary, thus making doctoral work more feasible. Hence, the Clinical Pharmaceutical Ph.D. program was created to reflect the demands of the discipline. The CSA program's goals are described as follows:

> The goals of this mechanism were to (1) provide a mentored clinical pharmacy experience; (2) allow for a clinical experience that coincides with the students' dissertation research to create synergy of learning; (3) offer clinical preceptor experience and didactic teaching opportunities; (4) foster relationships with physicians and other health-care professionals; and (5) provide a competitive part-time pharmacist salary (Tortorici, Skledar, Zemaitis, Weber, Smith, Kroboth, & Poloyac 2007, 2).

An investigation of the program revealed positive outcomes as a whole. The clinical experience component provided in CSA, although not present in many other graduate programs, provided an avenue for doctoral students to advance clinical knowledge and skills. In this instance, the school of pharmacy realized partnerships and collaboration opened up student opportunities that were not previously available.

The prospects for this level of collaboration are limitless in educational leadership programs. For example Hoyle and colleagues (2005) assert that a committee with a good balance between theoretical full-time faculty and part-time practicing school administrators serving as adjunct or clinical faculty take the graduate student "beyond the generalities normally found in education policy textbooks and stresses strategies for current and future CEOs to navigate the winding paths of school/community politics" (xi).

This blend of faculty enriches possibilities that includes creating research and practice collaborations with school districts and regional service agencies, enlisting support from key state and local educational agencies, and more fully integrating services provided through social agencies to ensure that students are ready to learn. Committees made up of representatives from these groups would ensure students are capturing the more comprehensive knowledge and skill base necessary to leading today's schools.

As Bjork and Ginsberg (1995) suggest, an emphasis on preparation for best practice "may lead to more collegial relationships between trainers of administrators and administrators themselves. Perhaps school districts working in combination with training programs would agree to paid internships or allow potential principals to be released from school-level duties to pursue training" (31).

While a design of thorough and sustained student support throughout the program may have promise, there is no assurance it will work in all settings. Such a change in committee purpose and design may not be acceptable to all members of a faculty who feel present practices have worked well and should not be changed and see the proposed change as unrealistic and idealistic given the scope of factors. In reality, a critical discussion around topics such as shared-decision making, meaningful collaboration, and perceptions of legitimate and useful field knowledge will need to occur if the work and function of the committees are to be redesigned.

The committee process must be structured and meet on a consistent basis for it to be effective. Consultation around students' academic and practical needs must occur at regular points throughout the course of a program. It is recommended that the committee along with the student develop an academic and professional growth plan when the student begins the program. The growth plan must include realizable and practicable objectives that can be evaluated and recorded. Tracking progress serves as a basis for subsequent committee meetings where advice and suggestions are given that support the student's advancement toward the goals of the growth plan.

As mentioned previously, programs will need resources of various kinds for this model of committee support to occur successfully. We feel students will benefit in a meaningful way through exposure to multiple perspectives about the needs of schools and the community. Thus, committees must consist of a diverse set of voices.

Necessary conditions noted by one report (Bottoms & O'Neill 2001) include: (a) establishing an advisory board consisting of faculty, field representatives, a state department of education representative, and other key community roles, (b) ensuring funding is available to support time, staffing, and other critical program aspects (c) soliciting legal or policy support from state agencies to facilitate implementation, (d) supporting tenured and tenure track faculty to engage in field-based research, and (e) rewarding school based efforts in the tenure and promotion process.

DEMONSTRATION OF KNOWLEDGE AND SKILLS: PERFORMANCE-BASED EVALUATION

We believe that students' development in the program should be assessed by student advisory committees using highly practical and authentic methods. This is not to suggest that traditional paper-based evaluations or inventories of knowledge have not been fruitful or that these features should be discarded. We envision a culminating activity that requires students demonstrate to the advisory committee knowledge and skills acquired using portfolios, literature and brochures, art, prose, mock scenarios and skits, and other nontraditional forms of evidence.

This approach has been used with great success by Teachers College Summer Principals Academy at Columbia University where students create schools that meet the needs of all children as a capstone activity. The portfolio offers promise as a cumulative record of learning experiences, field-based and academic projects written and performed, and other forms of data that reflect the professional capabilities of students. Mock scenarios or short skits may also reveal degrees of maturation or development in tacit elements of leadership that are not easily captured by paper-based questions.

If designed optimally, such an experience can yield valuable insight to the student, as well as the committee as far as the quality of preparation. In the highly interactive assessment, the student is continually challenged to demonstrate his or her preparation for leadership using the various devices previously mentioned. A genuine professional atmosphere is sought in order to replicate a real school setting that emphasizes the interplay between the technical realm of teaching and learning, politics, and culture.

Every effort is made by the committee chair and other members to prepare each future school administrator to address what Reis-Louis refers to as the three dimensions of change for any newcomer. As Reis-Louis argues (2001), change, contrast, and surprise are three dimensions that the newcomer usually confronts in a new culture. Transitioning to a new work role or setting (i.e., change) requires leaders know how to function with their role in the school organization, have knowledge of law and policy, have expertise in the technical core of schooling, and have the ability to manage a complex system.

In reality, newly appointed leaders in schools often are confounded by countless irrational aspects. The advisory committee is vital in advising newly minted leaders how to adapt to the cultural and political landscape of schools and ways to be aware of behaviors very different from those encountered in textbooks (i.e., contrast). The new leader discovers pockets of resistance, instructional skill deficits, and minimal adherence to rules and process among the teaching staff.

Unlike highly formal and mechanistic organizations, new principals learn abruptly that power in schools is not distributed in a rank-and-file manner. Schools contain complex informal systems that are difficult to discern. Disillusioned leaders are "surprised" by the contrast and search for reasons and factors to explain the dissonance. In response, new leaders render changes marginally effective or result in the opposite intended effect. Sadly, some leaders disheartened and frustrated by the experience will succumb to the surprising organizational conditions and reverse course in pursuing needed change that would certainly alter the status quo.

Other leaders, at their peril, will stand pat and show little tolerance for opposition that unexpectedly results in organizational mistrust and dissatisfaction. The committee chair is responsible to help the advisee to anticipate the reality that some schools will resist all efforts at change and improvement. For that reason, we feel the critical charge of the committee is to prepare students to face these challenges while at the same time develop leaders who stay the course in providing the best education for all children.

A major role of the committee chair is to ensure that students present evidence demonstrating their understanding of the theory and practice leadership. For practice, emphasis is given to the tacit and obscure elements of leadership presented previously. In addition to validating the individualization of leadership preparation and the inclusion of external members, this activity should serve as an opportunity for students to showcase practical skills such as conducting a mock faculty meeting where a proposal to modify an existing practice is introduced, developing an employee handbook, creating student/parent information packets, or addressing issues of race and culture to a campus and community.

All of these simulated projects or experiences provide useful evidence which in turn can be broadcasted within or outside the institution. For instance, a portfolio of the student's work could be posted on college's server so that it is accessible to potential employers. Information may include video recordings and written projects demonstrating preparation for the new demands and challenges of schools.

In the end, all committee members share responsibility for student learning and preparation. Quality is stressed throughout. In addition to academic mastery, committees prepare students to strive for equity and justice, manage conflict, and cope with the informal and highly unpredictable circumstances of schools. To review, it is important that committees make full use of the applied faculty and fully tap into their expertise of tacit field issues. Formal instruction, while valuable, provides only one dimension to leadership and must be supported by systematic field experiences coordinated by the program's clinical personnel.

Partnerships and other means to involving outside stakeholders in the process of leadership development are crucial and should be continually sought. As previously stressed, much remains to be learned about leadership and schools. Encouraging involvement and participation from outside personnel, such as school, community, and business leaders, can only enrich our knowledge of practice. Finally, graduate committee faculty should seek alternative ways for students to demonstrate their development as leaders. Performance-based presentations not only provide a clearer and more relevant indication of school leadership readiness but also a means to attracting potential employers.

HOW TO INCREASE THE VALUE OF GRADUATE COMMITTEES

As indicated previously, the advisory committee should take a major role in controlling for quality and guidance toward successful careers as principals or superintendents. Our observations find a variety of student advisory committees and their assigned or assumed duties. In addition, Web or brochure information infrequently mentions the advisory committee role or number of faculty on master's or doctoral student committees.

We suggest that each master's degree student's advisory committee should consist of two tenured faculty and one adjunct or clinical professor. As indicated, the adjunct professor is important in creating and monitoring a meaningful internship experience and infusing real world application into all course content and activities. The doctoral advisory committee should consist of three tenured and one clinical faculty member. Two of the tenured and the clinical members should be part of the educational leadership faculty and the third member should be in a related discipline within the college of education or in a related field of management, sociology, psychology, public service, or philosophy.

The doctoral committee chair is perhaps the most important person to the student and should be very carefully selected, if possible. The chair is the primary advisor and sometimes advocate to guide the student in creating the committee, developing the degree plan, preparing for and scheduling the comprehensive examination, preparing a research proposal, writing the dissertation, and helping to prepare the student for a successful final dissertation defense.

THE ROLE OF COMMITTEE CHAIR—MASTER'S DEGREE

The committee chair for master's degree students is responsible for guiding students in creating the degree plan and the requirements for state licensure, counseling the student when needed, and in many instances supervising field experience. In addition, the chair advises the student during the course work, checks progress on the degree plan, suggests ways to prepare for the final oral and written examinations, how to create a portfolio, and assists the student in pursuing an administrative position as a school leader. Also, the committee chair occasionally supervises a student's thesis for the Master of Science degree.

We suggest that holding an oral examination for the master's degree student is an important activity. Our experience with a variety of capstone exercises (i.e., portfolio, written examination, or research paper) is that while they are important, we find them inadequate in providing the advisory committee enough evidence to assess the student's potential for school leadership.

The final oral examination should be based on the student's course work in the core areas of school leadership, law, student learning, curriculum requirements, instructional processes, student performance assessment, and student auxiliary services. In order to narrow the scope of the oral examination, the chair should require each student to ask each committee member three weeks before the examination for advice on the types of questions each professor may pose. This process helps reduce some of the fear and tension of the examination and turns it into a positive learning experience.

The Master's Degree Oral Examination

The committee chair in collaboration with the student and department academic advisor should establish a date for the oral examination. The chair should contact the student at the beginning of the final semester of course work and discuss the process of contacting the other two committee members about what types of questions they may ask at the examination. Approximately three weeks before the agreed upon date, the chair contacts the academic advisor's office to set the date, time, and place for the one-and-one-half hour examination.

Three days before the final oral examination the chair should contact the academic advisor's office to assure that the official examination forms are available for the examination. Also, advise the student to e-mail or call the other two members one or two days before to remind them of the time and place. Once the committee and student arrive for the examination and greet each other, the chair then begins with introductions of committee members and the student.

Next, the chair begins the examination by asking the student to talk about his or her current job, family, and plans for the future. This brief time usually puts the student at ease before the questioning begins. The chair then asks one of the committee members to begin the examination, but the other committee member should feel free to ask the student for clarification. The same examination protocol should be followed with the other committee members and chair. When it is apparent that the examination has gone well, committee members should then turn to the chair and indicate that they have no further questions.

At this point, the chair asks the student to step out of the room for a few moments to allow the committee to talk. The chair then asks the other two members if the student's responses were acceptable. If the responses are positive, the chair then asks for signatures on the graduate school form indicated a pass. As soon as the signatures are secured the chair invites the student back into the room to receive congratulations for passing the final examination. If the student displays exceptional talent in both the content and communication, the committee may encourage the student to consider pursuing the doctoral degree.

In some instances, the student will fare poorly during the oral examination and fail to pass. In this case the committee will instruct the chair to talk with the student about retaking the exam and present the retake to the committee chair or the entire committee to assure the gaps have been addressed. The role of the chair becomes extremely important in the case of student failure on the final oral examination. They must assume the role of counselor, teacher, and communicator with the other two committee members about assignments and necessary progress made by the student toward graduation.

THE ROLE OF COMMITTEE CHAIR—DOCTORAL LEVEL

Beverly Martinez, a middle school principal, has decided to pursue her dream and apply for a doctoral program. She has served as a seventh grade language arts teacher for four years and after completing her master's degree and licensure was selected by her superintendent to become a middle school assistant principal. After two successful years as an assistant principal, Beverly was named middle school principal in another school within the district. The superintendent of her district earned his doctorate from the same large research-one university and was serving as an adjunct professor in educational leadership at a nearby regional university.

The superintendent invited professor Jennifer Collier, a faculty member from the regional university, to speak at their school district opening day convocation. Beverly was impressed with Dr. Collier's intellect, communication skills, and ability to relate to the problems her school was facing and after the session engaged her in a brief conversation about their doctoral program in educational leadership. Dr. Collier gave her a business card and invited Beverly to call her very soon and talk more about their doctoral program.

The next day at an administrator meeting, Beverly asked her superintendent to compare the quality of doctoral programs and faculty at the large university and Dr. Collier's regional university. The superintendent talked about the positives and negatives of each program but recommended the regional university because of its strong focus on preparing public school leaders and evidence of strong research and writing based on real school issues. He indicated that the strong link to public schools was because of the veteran faculty: most of the newer faculty members were graduates of research-one universities and all but two of them had served as school administrators previously in their careers.

He added that several of the faculty members were active at the state and national levels in principal and superintendent associations and cosponsored a very successful annual leadership academy with the state superintendent association. He told Beverly that she would gain more toward career advancement from the regional faculty since they were respected both by their scholarly peers and had name recognition by the school administrators in the state and nation. Beverly also sought more advice from graduates of both programs and decided to apply to the regional program.

After her admission to the Executive Leadership Ed. D. program, she asked if she could select her temporary advisor and if so she would be honored to work with Dr. Collier. The academic advisor advised Beverly that she would ask Dr. Collier because she was very popular with the students and already has a large number of advisees. Dr. Collier agreed to talk with Beverly about the possibility of agreeing to serve as temporary committee chair and they arranged for a time to meet.

The first meeting was about Beverly's life, family, current job, and future aspirations; Dr. Collier handed Beverly a five-page policy document that included important information. Beverly perused the document and then listened to Dr. Collier.

Temporary Faculty Advisor

Dr. Collier told Beverly that she would soon need to select a faculty member to serve as her temporary adviser and then within the first two years (thirty-six credit hours) select a permanent committee chair. The permanent chair can be the temporary advisor, but a student should not feel obligated to the temporary chair beyond the temporary appointment.

The selection of the committee chair will be the most crucial decision a student will make. For this reason, the student should meet as many faculty members as possible as early as possible in the program.

With the chairperson, students will select the remaining members of the advisory committee and complete the degree plan. The chair or co-chair and a second member must be faculty members within the program. At least one member of the committee must be from a department other than educational administration.

Degree Plan

The degree plan must be on file with the office of graduate studies prior to completing thirty-six semester credit hours. Failure to comply will result in a student being blocked from registration until a degree plan is on file. To complete the degree plan, a student must submit it online with the office of graduate studies and it will then be sent to all committee members and department representatives for electronic approval. The student will then be notified when the degree plan has been approved and on file with the office of graduate studies.

Admission to Candidacy

To be admitted to candidacy a student must have taken the pre-assessment exam, passed the preliminary exam, filed with the office of graduate studies the dissertation proposal approved by the advisory committee, competed the formal coursework, and completed residency requirement.

Residency Requirements for the Doctorate

Residency requirements for the Executive Leadership doctorate requires enrollment as a full-time student (minimum of nine credit hours per semester); the nine hours can be taken on campus—usually weekends or summer sessions or approximately 25 percent can be online—that also includes face-to-face meetings with classmates and the professor. While the residency requirement is flexible to meet the needs of full-time school executives, it is demanding and expects the student to spend considerable time in class, conducting research, and conversing with the committee chair about the dissertation or other scholarly projects.

Pre-Assessment Exam for Entering Doctoral Students

As recommended in Step Two, students are required to take the entry-level exam questions found on pages 53–54. As indicated, if the written response on any of the six essay questions is marginal the temporary advisor will then assign the student readings/activities recommended for each question found in Step Three, pages 78–81. This pre-assessment exam is highly recommended to help the committee chair assess both the writing and knowledge levels of all entry students.

The exam will be given a few weeks prior to the first semester to assist the chair in guiding a student in closing some knowledge gaps. This assessment will help assure that all members of the class or cohort will have comparable entry knowledge about the big issues in educational leadership.

Examinations

At or near the completion of course, the student will complete an oral and written preliminary exam prior to admission to candidacy for the doctoral degree. The student must have a grade point average of at least 3.0 when scheduling the exam. The exam is taken when he or she is within six hours of completing course work. Both the oral and written portions of the exam must be taken within a two-week period. Preliminary exams will not be scheduled during the summer semesters since numerous faculty are not available. The preliminary exam must be taken and results submitted at least fourteen weeks prior to the defense of the dissertation.

Proposal Presentation

The proposal hearing allows the student to finalize with the committee the details regarding the dissertation. The proposal must be submitted to the office of graduate studies at least fifteen days prior to the scheduled defense date of the dissertation. The committee chair works closely with the student in preparation of the proposal presentation. It is not uncommon for a student to rewrite part or the entire proposal several times before the chair agrees that the proposal is ready for review by the members of the committee.

While few proposals are perfect, the expectation for the meeting is that of a working session for the committee to help the student clarify the research plan and to assure high quality in the process. After advice from the committee, the student will prepare the revised document to the chair and in some cases to the other committee members. If the corrections are acceptable, the committee will sign a form indicating their approval for the student to begin the research process.

Submission of Institutional Review Board Protocol

The student is required to have approval to conduct his or her research prior to beginning collecting data. The proposal hearing must be held before submission of the Institutional Review Board (IRB) protocol for permission to conduct research involving human subjects. After the IRB papers are submitted to the IRB office, the student will be notified when he or she has been approved to begin collecting data.

Dr. Collier's Advice to Beverly about the Dissertation Process

Dr. Collier told Beverly that in the next eighteen months, if not before, the committee chair will begin guiding her toward creating the best possible dissertation. She has the responsibility to submit both hard and online copies first to her chair and then with the chair's approval she will send a hard and online copy to the all committee members and thank them for all their help. Also she will inform them that she will check with them in two weeks and ask them if they have any concerns about the study.

If the committee members agree that the study is ready to defend then the defense date is set two weeks hence. The student should hand the dissertation to committee members and inform them that the student and his or her chair would like to set a defense date in two weeks. Once the time and date are set, it is the student's responsibility to inform an academic advisor so that a letter of announcement can be processed.

The committee chair and department head must sign the letter of announcement. The announcement of the defense must be submitted to the office of graduate studies at least ten working days prior to the scheduled date. Before the final defense the student should arrange a conference with the thesis office so that their document can be reviewed for formatting and other requirements.

Because of the required signatures, the academic advisor should be notified at least three weeks prior to the scheduled final defense date. In addition, the student should submit to all committee members in final form the dissertation three weeks prior to the scheduled defense date. Letters are sent to all committee members announcing the date and time of each exam. It is strongly recommended that the student contact all committee members the day before each exam to ensure that they will be present.

At least one week before the defense date prepare at ten- to fourteen-slide PowerPoint presentation that includes the title, introduction, problem statement, purpose of the study, research questions/hypotheses, research procedures and methods, research findings, conclusions (linked to the theoretical framework), and recommendations. Also the student should prepare hard copies of the power point and additional pages that include any changes suggested by committee members during the prior two weeks. These changes plus others that emerge during the defense will be incorporated into the final copy.

When the dissertation is successfully defended, a single copy of the approval page needs to be brought to the thesis office, and instructions will be provided regarding the electronic submission of the dissertation. The student should have the approval page at the final defense so that committee members' signatures can be obtained.

While Beverly knew that she would not remember the details of creating and defending a dissertation, she did gain a broader perspective of the work to be done to be called "Dr." After listening carefully to the detailed description of the reading material and about the dissertation process, Beverly asked Dr. Collier to serve as her temporary advisor and she agreed. Beverly scored well on the pre-assessment exam and scheduled sessions twice a month for the next two years with Dr. Collier to stay on track with the degree plan, attended weekend, online, evening, and summer classes while conducting online and library research required to create a successful research proposal.

After completion of all course work, Beverly worked closely with her committee to prepare and pass her preliminary comprehensive examination. Since she had settled on a dissertation topic during her second semester, she got her proposal approved by her committee and the IRB committee to begin gathering the necessary data during the summer of her second year. Dr. Collier worked closely with Beverly to complete a high quality study and took deliberate steps to assure that the other three committee members had plenty of time to read and respond to Beverly about her study.

Dr. Collier provided timely feedback to Beverly and guided her in securing feedback from the other committee members. After all committee suggestions to improve the document were completed, the dissertation defense date was set three weeks in advance. After a successful defense of her study and additional corrections to her study, Beverly completed all requirements and asked Dr. Collier to "hood" her at graduation. She is now Dr. Beverly Martinez.

Dr. Collier's Advice to Dissertation Chairs

The creation and completion of a doctoral dissertation is often surrounded with fear and mystery. Completing and defending a dissertation is arguably the most stressful activity for students and professors of educational leadership. Emotions emerging while chairing a dissertation range from the exhilaration of hooding the new doctoral student to the frustrations of correcting poor writing, rereading, and requiring the student to redo major portions of a chapter, instructing the student to distribute the several times reworked document to other committee members, and waiting on their feedback before attempting to set the final defense date. This stress is compounded if the professor is also chairing four or five more dissertations simultaneously.

Therefore, we offer our colleagues the following advice.

First: Not surprisingly, some students are easier to chair than others. In a perfect world we would serve as dissertation chairs for only the best and brightest students. It is no secret that the best writers and students smooth the dissertation journey for the chair, other committee members and the student. However, the world remains imperfect and we as servant leaders during our weaker moments agree to serve as chair for those who need our guidance. The problem of guiding some students is like swimming upstream—once you begin swimming, the current of weak writing skills and waves of inadequate research methods becomes a journey of survival for you and the student.

We find that requiring students with weak writing skills to enroll in a writing course improves their basic skills. Also, requiring the student to purchase *Elements of Style* by William Strunk is another source for improving writing skills. Some students with strong writing skills like Beverly make us appear to be better than we are while other ones challenge us beyond out capacities. As a result of these thrills and disappointments, we have suggested in faculty meetings many times the admission criteria should be strengthened to include students capable of completing a dissertation.

Second: Dissertation chairs must be taskmasters on the design of the research prospectus or proposal. A solid theoretical framework, research problem, purpose and research questions, and clear procedures and selected methods solve 80 percent of the stress of supervision. Poorly designed proposals lead to distress for both professor and student. A chair and committee should never approve a proposal that lacks a clear focus for data gathering, analysis, and contribution to the knowledge base of the field.

Once we have signed a poorly devised proposal we are swimming on that upstream journey for a long time. Agreeing to approve a weak proposal also places a chair in an uncomfortable position with the other committee members who may decide that the study has little promise and refuse to sign the approval form.

Third: Close communication between the student and chair is paramount. Once the data gathering is underway, the student must stay in close contact about the process. Ask the student about any difficulties in data gathering such as percentage of returns on self-report questionnaires or issues around interviews with research subjects and what is the percentage of return of the questionnaires from the research subjects and issues around interviews with research subjects.

Poor communication between the chair and the student is a primary reason that details can go awry in data collection, analysis, and connections to the theory base. During the dissertation writing process, expect the student to contact you at least once every two weeks and make sure you share phone numbers, mailing addresses, Facebook, and e-mail addresses. Easy access to each other reduces much frustration in the communication process.

Fourth: Get help with the data analysis. If you as chair lack the expertise in the quantitative or qualitative method, seek help from colleagues in or out of the department. Calling on the help of a colleague on the committee within the department to assist the student with methods beyond our memory or preparation helps assure a high quality product. Even if we feel comfortable with the methodology, it is good to check our memory in order to better advise the student and avoid complications at the final defense. Most doctoral students pass their required methods courses, but applying what was mastered in class usually falls short at dissertation time.

Fifth: Be patient with other committee members. To expect the other members of the committee to jump right on to reading your dissertation is daydreaming. They are preparing for classes, advising students, consulting in public schools, reading their own advisees' dissertations, and producing or rewriting their own scholarly papers and books. Busy faculty have a professional duty to read and react to the student's dissertation, but usually push it to the back of the desk or pass through the e-mail attachment.

For this reason the committee chair must charge the student to produce a well-written scholarly tome that the other committee members find organized and readable. Our experience tells us that three or four readings of the entire document is standard and close scrutiny of the findings and conclusions sections is mandatory before asking the student to share copies with the other committee members.

Sixth: Set flexible timelines for the committee. We suggest that the student submit both an e-mail attachment and a hard copy of the dissertation to all committee members, including the chair. The student will send an e-mail or hard copy memorandum with the dissertation asking the committee to (please) review the document in twelve to fifteen working days. The memorandum should indicate that if no significant problems are found with the study a tentative final defense date will be approximately two weeks after the twelve- to fifteen-day review period.

This timeline helps reduce the pressure on committee members and allows them time to read the study and contact the chair about any major problems. Perhaps the problems can be rectified in time for the defense. However, if the problem is of a more serious nature, the chair will instruct the student and inform the committee about a later date for the defense. These flexible timelines have proven to be less stressful and more conducive to helping the student produce a higher quality dissertation. After following a flexible and collegial process of working with the student and the committee members, the dissertation defense is in most cases a success for the student.

In some instances during the student defense, a committee member may choose to go beyond reasonable questions to negative criticism of the document. If this occurs, the chair can explain that the student followed the instructions of each committee member who agreed that the dissertation was acceptable for the defense. If the committee member is greatly concerned about the research methods or procedures the chair can remind the committee that the methods and procedures were approved by the committee at the proposal hearing and should have little bearing on the final document.

If the committee member's concerns cannot be appeased by the chair while the student is present, ask the student to leave the room before continuing committee deliberations. If the problem can be resolved within a reasonable time frame, the chair will invite the student back to the defense. If the problem cannot be resolved, inform the committee that the defense will be rescheduled in the near future and appropriate steps will be taken by the chair to work with the committee member and require the student to make additions or corrections to the document and then set another defense date.

The Critical Roles of Committee Members

Again the importance of the student advisory committee cannot be overestimated. An advisory committee has two primary functions. First, the committee chair with committee approval guides the student in creating an acceptable degree plan inclusive of the discipline of educational administration and outside courses important to the roles of principal and superintendent.

The master's committee chair is the primary advisor for the students' degree plan and licensure requirements, but the other two members also play important roles in advising the student about skills and knowledge needed for school leadership. In addition, all committee members are vital in planning a valuable final exam for students, assisting them in acquiring their first administrative job, and in some instances encouraging the student to consider applying for a doctoral program.

The doctoral committee chair and committee members hold the future of every advisee in their academic hands. The student's welfare must be primary in all decisions blended with a touch of tough love to keep them on track. If the admission criteria are carefully applied to the selection of students into the program then the committee should take the collective stance that the student will successfully complete the program.

A doctoral student at the University of Colorado told a frightened new classmate who was stressing about the overwhelming requirement of the program to remember "If they let you in they have to let you out!" Those comforting words from a classmate helped that scared student remain in the program and build an outstanding career of scholarship in educational administration.

Therefore, the doctoral committee chair becomes a most significant mentor to their students. The bonding between the chair and the student is inevitable and can be troubling to the chair when the advisee does not perform well on the preliminary exam or the dissertation defense. While we may have a tendency to smooth the path for our advisees, we must remember that the student moves on, but your colleagues do not.

While the welfare of the student is paramount, the committee chair must remain very objective and respect the concerns that the other committees have about the quality level of the advisee's performances. All of us remember the influence of our doctoral committee chair. The authors of this book would not have succeeded without the caring leadership of our advisors Dr. Paul R. Hensarling, Dr. William Boyd, and Dr. Jacqueline Stefkovich.

6

Step Five

Creating and Maintaining an Effective Support Staff

Three outstanding staff members have been selected to represent the many outstanding employees often overlooked as key players in most departments of leadership education. They are Joyce Nelson, senior academic advisor at Texas A&M University; Maureen Hoatson, administrative assistant to the Chair at Seton Hall University; and Becky Contestabile, staff assistant at Pennsylvania State University. These three talented and tireless workers represent over four hundred key staff serving as senior academic advisors or office assistants to school leadership preparation programs.

In the smaller programs in terms of student enrollment, these key staff members must be multitaskers who assume other responsibilities that include payroll, budgets, travel arrangements, office equipment, computers, and correspondence of various types. These support staff members are dedicated leaders who attend to the daily needs of the department and provide vital links between graduate and undergraduate students, faculty, and the university admissions and degree requirements.

Many times, they are the face of the department for most master's and doctoral students and are ambassadors in the university and community. Potential graduate students' first impression of a program in educational administration is frequently measured by how well they are received when they walk into a department office or place a phone call inquiring about the program.

The Nelsons, Haotsons, and Contestabiles of the leadership preparation world are usually the initial contact for prospective students. They help process their admissions material, schedule admissions interviews, coordinate interview teams, and collect and oversee faculty assessment of students' writing exercises. They supervise or prepare criteria tabulations for faculty review and conduct student admissions meetings with the faculty. Next, they help prepare admit or deny letters for each applicant. The students report to these writers that these friendly, caring, and skilled advisors often kept them from dropping out of their degree programs.

Without these talented people, who would assure that students receive assistance with registration, degree plans, petitions, Q-drops, withdrawals, change of grades, and curriculum forms? They also help monitor student progress (Grade Point Ratio) and build the class schedules both on and off campus, for the Trans-Texas Video Conference Network (TTVN), and for online courses. In some cases they keep payroll records for graduate students on assistantships, scholarships, fellowships, and grants.

Other primary roles these valuable assistants play include maintaining classroom utilization reports, communicating with the office of graduate studies, and preparing paperwork for students' exams and final defenses. They attend faculty meetings, administer semester grade sheets, and pride themselves as being a positive liaison between students, faculty, and university offices and personnel. They oversee new student orientation that may include snacks or lunches and invite faculty members to provide brief reviews of their areas of teaching expertise. They also monitor the difficult task of principal and superintendent certification requirements and state examinations and maintain communications on these licensure issues with the dean's office.

A STUDENT'S ASSISTED JOURNEY THROUGH A MASTER'S DEGREE

Gloria Sanders, a former eighth grade teacher is now an assistant principal in the same school. Three years earlier she decided to pursue her master's degree in educational administration and work her way toward the position of principal. Before applying for the master's degree, Gloria recalls talking with others pursuing the same goal and with her principal about her potential as an assistant principal on her campus or within the school district. After positive comments on her administrative potential, Gloria e-mailed the senior academic advisor at the regional state university about the admissions process.

The advisor sent a program description and application to Gloria and told her to return her information within the month in order to prepare the materials in time for the next faculty admissions committee. The admissions form requested Gloria's undergraduate grade point average, teaching experience, GRE or MAT scores, three recommendation forms completed by current employers and former professors, and a two-page personal philosophy of education. After receiving Gloria's application and completed recommendation forms, the academic advisor compiled her information on a master list that included several other applicants.

The academic advisor asked two faculty members to grade Gloria's philosophy of education using a ten-point scoring scale. After all the applicants' data were recorded, packets were prepared for faculty for their review. Next, in collaboration with the program chair, the academic advisor scheduled a two-hour admissions meeting. Gloria's evaluation was positive and a faculty member agreed to chair her committee and guide her into the proper classes.

Soon after the admission meeting, Gloria remembers a very successful event planned by the academic advisor. She planned a four-hour orientation session for new graduate students that included a detailed explanation about the mysteries of online course scheduling, ID numbers, library access, parking, tuition and fees, and other important details to help reduce the fear of the unknown. Lunch was brought in and faculty members welcomed and mixed with the new students to share their areas of academic interests. Gloria found this orientation very helpful and reduced some of the tension about the academic challenges, faculty, staff, and her future classmates.

They were told about the committee structure that includes the chair and two more faculty members who are added after two semesters. One of the members is selected from within the leadership education faculty and the second member from another area (i.e., curriculum, technology, educational psychology). Some leadership education programs include faculty in one or more of the "outside areas" to help simplify the committee selection process.

Since Gloria was a full-time teacher, she could attend classes only in the evenings or on weekends and was advised to take two classes each semester, a mini-semester class in December, and two or three classes during the summer session. One of the summer classes in curriculum was offered online, which helped save driving time to campus. Several weeks before the first semester began, Gloria met with the academic advisor and responded to the LSI to determine her level of actual participation toward mastering the thirty-one functions linked to the six 2008 *Educational Leadership Policy Standards: ISLLC.*

Gloria remembers feeling very inadequate to complete the LSI since she had been a classroom teacher for seven years and the only administrative knowledge she had came from chairing the campus site-based team that included issues of personnel, budget, and curriculum. Thus, the obvious gaps in her LSI scores were indicative of her limited experiences in leadership or management. The academic advisor assured Gloria that she was not expected to master these areas at the beginning of her program.

The results indicated that she had participated very little in four of the functions under standard 1; very little or moderately in two of the functions in standard 2; very little on four of the five functions in standard 3 that emphasizes management operations; moderate participation on two of the functions under standard 4; moderate participation on two of the functions for standard 5; and very little participation on two of the functions under standard 6. Based on this assessment the faculty advisor sent a copy of Gloria's LCI assessment to the academic advisor who filed the pretest scores and later her posttest scores at the completion of course work and internship experiences.

Gloria remembers that each required course aligned with specific standards and functions, and her faculty advisor and the academic advisor reviewed the LCI posttest for any glaring gaps in the knowledge or experiential base of the state licensure examination. If gaps had remained in Gloria's knowledge base, her faculty advisor would have assigned specific readings found in Step Three of this book in order to assure that all functions had been addressed or reinforced.

Each of Gloria's classes included a required field research or evaluation project linked to relevant standards and functions that was submitted to the campus principal and the faculty advisor. This project was closely monitored by the faculty advisor who arranged two sessions on the school campus with Gloria and the principal.

Along with the project Gloria was required to attend and record two school board meetings, shadow her principal for a period of four weeks that included early morning leadership team staff meetings in the central office. Gloria's research project was suggested as a need by the superintendent and principal because they needed findings from the most recent research and best practices on inclusion of special needs students into various levels of math and science.

During Gloria's final semester, the academic advisor and the faculty committee chair arranged a final oral examination. The three-person committee reviewed Gloria's academic record and LCI scores before the examination. The questioning process began with the committee chair asking Gloria to talk about her career, family, and future aspirations as an educator. This was a good tension reducer for her, and it gave the committee greater insights into her personal and professional life and future dreams. The questions asked by the committee were based on the course work, internship experiences, and assigned readings related to the course content and standards and functions.

Gloria remembers being very nervous but addressed each of the questions reasonably well and passed the examination with honors. The committee recommended that she continue her graduate studies after she receives her state principal license and lands her first administrative position. The committee chair encouraged Gloria to apply in three school districts with assistant principal openings and the chair agreed to follow up by contacting former students serving as personnel directors, principals, and superintendents.

Gloria served in the classroom one more year and was selected as an assistant principal in the school where she taught. She finds the administrative life challenging and has applied for the doctoral program in the same university. She plans to complete the doctorate and seek a position as principal or systems administrator in the area of curriculum or personnel. Gloria now says, "I had a dream the other night about being a superintendent and it was not a nightmare." Gloria will no doubt be a superintendent in the coming years.

A DOCTORAL STUDENT'S ASSISTED JOURNEY

Dr. Jeff Badgett is in his second year as a superintendent of a medium-sized school district of 5,600 students. Six years earlier he decided that his promotions possibilities from the small 1,298-student school district to a medium-sized district were remote. At that point, Jeff decided he needed a doctorate in order to compete for a medium-sized district with over 5,000 students. Jeff believed that he was prepared to seek such a role and applied for three jobs.

In his past experiences, he was either eliminated in the first screening or was in the final three with two candidates holding a doctorate. Jeff earned his bachelor's degree from a small liberal arts college and his master's degree from the state's largest and most prestigious university. He taught history and English and coached football and baseball for six years before earning the master's and principal certification. Then Jeff was ready for a new role and was hired as a high school principal in a small town twenty miles away. After five successful years leading the high school to high academic performance, Jeff applied and became superintendent where he had served as teacher and coach.

Jeff recalls taking his school board to a state convention six years earlier and coming across a booth sponsored by a research-one university displaying information about graduate degrees in educational leadership. The materials caught his eye and the academic advisor and a senior professor at the booth introduced themselves and talked with him about the new selective Executive Leadership Ed.D. for current or aspiring superintendents. The senior faculty member was well known throughout the state by superintendents and policy makers and had chaired dissertations for a few of Jeff's superintendent or university professor friends.

Jeff decided to visit the campus to meet with the academic advisor and the professor. He applied and with the exception of a marginal GRE combined score, his successful record in turning around a school district with over 60 percent of the students living below the poverty line made him a likely candidate. Also, he was viewed as a servant leader in community, church, and civic volunteer roles.

The professor contacted one of Jeff's former professors, two of his current school board members, and several teachers in his district about his interpersonal skills and service to others. After reviewing the materials and rankings with other new applicants and the report by the Professor, the faculty admitted Jeff to the Ed.D. Executive Leadership doctorate. Within a week, the senior academic advisor, after conversing with faculty, assigned each of the Ed.D. students to a faculty advisor.

Next, the academic advisor conducted a new doctoral student orientation for the new Ed.D. cohort and new students enrolling into the Ph.D program. The orientation included degree requirements and the few differences in research methods and types of residency for the Ph.D. students. Several faculty said that the Ed.D. is a professional degree of the highest quality designed to produce visionary leaders, reflecting thinkers, problem solvers, and excellent school executives. They also explained that this degree, while designed for practicing school leaders, also prepares graduates like Jeff to teach in higher education.

The curricula for the Ed.D. and Ph.D. are similar, but research requirements for the Ed.D. place greater emphasis on problem-based learning and skills to analyze and solve real-world school problems. After a complete presentation about course requirements, tuition, fees, faculty committee structures, and weekend, evening, and online classes in educational administration and related fields, lunch was delivered and the faculty joined the students for food and conversation.

Jeff's meeting with his advisor was very positive and helped answer some of the questions that he failed to ask at the new student orientation. The senior academic advisor also provided valuable advice about degree requirements and the course schedule for the next two academic years. While most of the classes were held on Fridays and Saturdays, there were also courses offered in the evenings or online in cognate areas. Jeff spent the rest of the day responding to the six question pretest (see Step Two).

Within one week the professor e-mailed Jeff that he had a grade of excellent on questions 1 and 4; good on questions 3 and 2, but marginal on questions 5 and 6. As a result of his poor performance on questions 5 and 6, the professor assigned four readings linked to the two questions found in Step 3. Two weeks later Jeff met with his professor and passed an oral examination on the two questions. With that accomplishment, he was ready for his first two doctoral classes in Organizational Theory and

Leadership in Education and Advanced Models for Managing High Performing Educational Systems.

Two years quickly passed as Jeff attended weekend or night classes, leading his small school system through some crises and trying to recruit "fully qualified" teachers to his rural school district. The process went smoothly thanks to reminders from the academic advisor and his committee chair. Also, the other three committee members were very helpful in assisting Jeff through the comprehensive written and oral examinations at the end of year two.

The committee chair helped Jeff identify an "action research" study during his first year and a proposal was approved by the committee at near the end of his second year. Jeff collected the data from the state data system and conducted a study on the role of superintendents in high-performing, cost-effective school districts. Jeff met his professor at the state and national superintendent's conventions, and those conversations helped increase his confidence that he could finish the dissertation and accomplish his dreams to be superintendent of a larger school district.

Jeff often called or e-mailed his academic advisor. She was indeed his savior during his doctoral studies. Her kindness in answering questions, in solving what appeared to be major problems with the office of graduate studies, and with the many deadlines students face in such programs smoothed the way. Every member of the cohort had great respect for this advisor because she understood the struggles they faced attempting to run a school or a school district and meet the rigors of doctoral study.

As indicated, conducting new master's and doctoral student orientation demands a lot of communication skill, hand-holding, and patience. Our staff, under the leadership of Joyce Nelson and Avery Pavliska at Texas A&M University, has created a very effective new student orientation PowerPoint presentation that may assist your staff.

They include instructions on the following:

1. How to register online.
2. How to pay online.
3. How to acquire a university ID number and e-mail account.
4. How to obtain a student ID.
5. When and how to submit a degree plan (i.e., master's student must submit degree plan before completing fifteen credit hours, and doctoral students must submit degree plan before completing thirty-six credit hours).
6. The students are provided with a department handbook/CD.
7. Assigning a temporary or initial advisor and a complete committee before submitting the degree plan.

8. Advice on selecting a committee chair and committee members—three members for master's and four members for the doctorate.
9. Instructions on how to purchase textbooks.
10. How to gain access to the student computer lab.
11. Invitations to be active in the Graduate Representative Advisory Board.
12. Access to library computers and key librarians.
13. Parking permits.

This PowerPoint presentation is available on the web: eahr.tamu.edu.

Other Key Staff Members

We have not ignored the role of other key players that help graduate programs run on time. Often the senior academic advisor may also wear the hat of business assistant or office assistant. In smaller programs, a skilled person may be capable of answering the phone, handling graduate admissions, scheduling, appointments, maintaining and ordering office supplies and equipment, and working as a liaison between fiscal, payroll, purchasing, contracts and grants, and retail vendors. Staff demands grow with student enrollments and new faculty hires. For every five new graduate students and two new faculty members, the office staff should consider hiring another worker. Otherwise the demands will increase beyond the staff's abilities and time.

In many programs student workers are hired to answer the phone, operate standard equipment, log faxes, maintain some departmental files, travel and leave requests, and other forms. In the larger doctoral programs (larger in terms of numbers of graduate students), the staff should consist of a general office manager who works closely with the department chair on faculty and graduate assistant issues and oversees department budget, faculty files, and stays connected to the college and university policies and transactions.

In addition, the larger programs need a senior office assistant who serves as a receptionist, supervises, trains, and evaluates the work of student workers, provides administrative support for specialized activities and projects, and plans logistical and administrative support for events, meetings, or other special functions.

For larger programs, more help is needed with the business side of the organization. A person either full- or part-time is needed to reconcile accounts on a monthly basis, process payments on items purchased for the department through the fiscal office, purchasing department, and directly with other companies. Of vital importance is this person's role in working as a liaison between fiscal, payroll, purchasing, contracts, and grants.

Also, this person's role includes making reservations for faculty and prospective employees with rental car agencies, airlines, and hotels. Most veteran administrators will tell you that you lose your job by being weak in two areas: interpersonal skills and finance. Thus, programs that prepare exemplary principals and superintendents must have a strong support staff with the interpersonal skills of a saint and management skills of a superintendent to keep the shop running in an efficient and timely manner.

While Step Five emphasizes the vital role of the academic advisors in attracting and communicating with graduate students and faculty, we have also included our thoughts on the valuable roles of receptionists, business assistants, and office managers. Regardless of the complexities of smooth office operation, the most valuable people are those who help attract and advise graduate students during their pursuit of a degree and support faculty in assuring that the programs are of the highest quality in academic rigor and relevance to the real challenges faced by current and future principals and superintendents.

In conducting external reviews of graduate programs in educational administration, we find that indicators of quality are linked to the attitudes and efficiency of the office staff. The annual graduate school rankings by U.S News and World Report should consider including another point category for the effectiveness of the office staff.

7

Step Six

Conducting Annual Reviews with Graduates Serving as Principals or Superintendents

Student evaluation of courses and instructors is a reality in higher education worldwide. Calls for greater accountability in higher education have increased the attention given to student evaluations of teaching effectiveness. While most student evaluations of faculty effectiveness are conducted at the end of the course rather than three or five years after the students are in the workforce, the results are both useful and controversial. Some end-of-course evaluations provide helpful feedback to the instructors, but some studies find that the personality and popularity of the professors rather than course content distort the accuracy of the evaluations.

Therefore, some observers believe that past or present students are incapable of judging the appropriateness of assignment, lectures, or examinations. However, in spite of the controversy, most current administrators and faculty find that student ratings and evaluations are valuable as determinants of teaching effectiveness (Jahangiri, Mucciolo, & Spielman 2008).

For this book we have little doubt that an ongoing feedback evaluation system is extremely important for annual adjustments to programs preparing principals and superintendents for schools in the United States. The greatest gap in leadership education preparation and research is the relationship between the preparation of principals and superintendents and their effectiveness in improving school and student performance.

We have survey after survey about the relevance of preparation and successful behaviors of administrative leadership, but questions linger about the program's impact on student achievement. Researchers discuss the futility in finding direct links between administrator behaviors and student performance. Researchers claim that too many complex variables and people are between the students and the administrators to isolate direct impacts.

According to Waters, Marzano, and McNulty (2003), the search for the missing link between administrators and student achievement has been underway for many years. They write that "[s]ince the early 1970s, many thoughtful, experienced, and competent scholars and practitioners have offered theories, anecdotes, and personal perspectives concerning educational leadership. None of this advice for leaders, however, was derived from the analyses of a large sample of quantitative data" (2).

A series of studies by Mid-continent Research for Education and Learning (McREL) seeking relationships between principal and superintendent impact on school improvement offer promise. The conclusions are drawn from meta-analyses of quantitative research on teacher, school, and leadership practices associated with student achievement. They provide evidence that if specific behaviors or responsibilities are performed by principals and superintendents, schools could improve. The findings reveal that for superintendents there are six district-level leadership responsibilities with a statistically significant relationship to student achievement.

The research on principals isolated twenty-one responsibilities that impact student learning. They found an average correlation *(r)* between district-level leadership behavior and achievement of 0.24. This means that a one standard deviation increase in district-level leadership is associated with a 9.5-percentile point difference in mean student achievement (Waters 2007). For campus-level principals they found a substantial relationship between leadership and student achievement. The average effect size between leadership and student achievement is 0.25. This means that this increase in leadership ability would translate into mean student achievement at one school with good leadership to be 10-percentile points higher than other schools with less effective leadership.

While these findings offer promise to our stumbling in the dark about how to prepare leaders to directly impact student achievement, there remain many gaps between how we prepare leaders who can directly impact student achievement. Thus, a key aspect is discovering how well leadership education helps our students become successful in leading schools to higher performance. Thus, this step, conducting annual reviews of our graduates is critical in finding the missing piece of the puzzle.

What are the perceptions of our graduates about the overall quality and relevance to actual practice of their school leadership preparation programs? Gwen Schroth and Anita Pankake (1999) asked their graduates in educational administration to assess the value of their learning to leading their schools or school districts. While they reported little value in taking exams, writing papers, and reading, they did find great value in resume writing and mock job interviews. Agreed this is not the feedback professors welcome, but it is important feedback from practicing school administrators.

Memories fade in time about the details of graduate study, but the perceptions of those currently serving as principals and superintendents are a valuable piece of the preparation puzzle. There is nothing new about graduate programs in leadership preparation conducting exit interviews, and in some cases, follow-up questionnaires are sent to graduates serving in leadership positions. The problems come in locating the former students and asking the right questions about the value of courses taken in years past.

Also, if the feedback is a collection of incoherent or scattered remarks, faculty members find little solid evidence to convince them to make changes in the programs. Brenda Graham (2007) conducted a study to determine if practicing school leaders in a doctoral program in Northeastern Pennsylvania believed their current and prior leadership education prepared them for leadership in their roles as school administrators. They were asked the following questions:

1. Do you think that your educational leadership program prepared you for present day school issues (standards, data analysis, accountability, diversity, etc.)?
2. What do you think are the most serious issues facing K–12 educational administration today?
3. What courses do you feel should be included in administrative/supervisory programs at colleges and universities?
4. What and how are you preparing your teachers for the changing demographics in your school?
5. Is this program (or any aspect of it) helping you to prepare your schools for the changing demographics (culturally and linguistically diverse students)?

While the study consisted of only fourteen doctoral students in an educational administration program, the findings are pertinent to this sixth step. Significantly the respondents indicated that their educational leadership preparation program adequately prepared them for their present administrative job and those who graduated with a master's degree after 1999 agreed that their programs adequately prepared them for the changing needs of twenty-first century schools. Those who graduated before 1999 felt that their programs did not stress many of today's reforms and stringent accountability issues. Graham provided the following recommendations for program adjustments:

1. A "Special Education" content course should be included in all educational leadership programs.

2. Knowledge of the experiences and academic needs of diverse groups of students (race, ethnicity, and socioeconomic) should be integrated throughout the program and factored into course planning.
3. Field experiences should engage the candidates in developing school problem-solving competencies.
4. Practical field experiences should be incorporated into school law courses.
5. Problem-based experiences should be incorporated into all classes.
6. Schools of education should work with the district and state policy makers to provide continuous postgraduate professional training for K–12 school leaders to keep them abreast of research and changes in the practice (Graham 2007, 47).

This small group of school leaders working toward their doctorates asserted that the content they were currently receiving in their doctoral program provided opportunity for them to "reflect on and discuss the leadership behaviors that are essential for meeting school improvement needs" (Graham 2007, 46). Thus, while suggestions were made for improvement, these students were positive about the relevance of past and current studies to the jobs they hold.

In a related study Hoyle and Oates (2000) found student evaluations of a Professional Studies Model (PSM) doctoral program at Texas A&M University were very positive and created adjustments in the new program. The purpose of the study was to investigate the relationship between the curriculum in the PSM and the professional development needs of those who have completed or are currently enrolled in the program.

A fifteen-item forced-choice and open-ended Doctoral Cohort Questionnaire was developed and mailed to forty-two former or current cohort members. Most of the students in the cohort perceived their programs to be "relevant, sensitive to their personal and professional lives, and academically rigorous" (Hoyle & Oates 2000, 107). They suggested that the statistics courses should be offered before the education research courses; that more emphasis is needed on program evaluation and data analysis; courses with more school visitation would be productive and that there was too much emphasis on preparation for the superintendency when more emphasis on instructional leadership is needed.

The results of this first comprehensive evaluation of the past and current PSM doctorate at Texas A&M University produced valuable data to assist faculty in improving the program. The impressions formed by those who have completed the program proved helpful. However, after data analysis the researchers realized that the questionnaire was inadequate to fully answer the professional development question.

Only four items were directed to the primary focus of the study, thus leaving the researchers and the reader asking more questions about the value of the cohort model in assisting the student in professional growth and success on the job. That is, more was needed in guiding the graduates toward creating schools and school systems focused on student achievement.

Another research project conducted by Jim Henderson (1995) at Duquesne University to gather perceptions of doctoral students and graduates of the Doctoral Program for Educational Leaders (IDPEL). The curriculum was based on the *AASA Professional Standards for the Superintendency* (Hoyle 1993). He found that students perceived the program to be relevant to their needs and praised the faculty for their willingness to commute to their home sites and their ease of communication with distance learning via satellite TV, e-mail, the Web, and video conferencing.

However, the findings were limited about the impact of the program on actual school improvement of student learning. A longitudinal study of a principal-cohort leadership academy at Bowling Green University revealed high ratings to the program on annual evaluations. Ninety percent of the graduates indicated they either held an administrative position or planned to seek one within the next five years. However, some agreed the adjunct professors focused too much on the managerial aspects of administration and too little on "the more recent focus of student outcomes and learning" (Zimmerman, Bowman, Valentine, & Barnes 2004, 235).

These worthwhile surveys gathering data from current and former students are valuable to program planners of master's and doctoral degrees. Overall students' responses in these studies are overwhelmingly positive about the courses, professors, and course scheduling. However, data about the relationship between the program quality and its impact on the graduates' success in improving school performance and student achievement are practically silent.

We believe that the value of well-designed surveys that provide valid feedback from former students is equal to the latest qualitative and quantitative research articles and books by their colleagues in higher education. Without former student feedback, our programs may jump on the latest jargon and methods gleaned from our fellow professors and lose our balance between scholarship and its impact on practice. We must be in constant dialogue with our graduates doing the real work with children and communities.

Although preparation standards continue to provide a minimum foundation for redesigning preparation, professors must indicate how their programs align with emerging global, national, state, and local social contexts. Preparation programs must redesign the curriculum to focus on the changing work of principals and superintendents. This ongoing evolution of curriculum and other teaching and learning experiences requires an understanding of global, national, and local contexts, as well as an administrator's role in aligning schools and districts with these emerging realities.

Our preparation programs must focus on how management and leadership skills can be brought to bear on the central tasks of improving student learning and building the capacity for shared leadership to sustain long-term change with a stronger sense of community. Also, leadership preparation must help our graduates effectively embed learning in work contexts and apply the latest most effective technologies. These skills must be taught to assure that our graduates can effectively attend to both the acquisition of knowledge and its application to higher performance for all students.

Each year we need to improve communication between professors in educational administration and our graduates serving as principals and superintendents. Prior to 1980 the literature reports a closer relationship between departments of educational administration and school administrators. Most faculty members attended and presented at state and national administrator conferences (i.e., AASA, NASSP, National Association of Elementary School Principals [NAESP], and ASCD) and were invited as consultants and visitors in schools and school districts and were selected for state and national advisory boards for professional administrator organizations to help bridge the gaps between professors and school administrators.

In 1979, the University Council for Educational Administration appointed a Partnership Coordinating Committee consisting of four professors and four major city superintendents. This committee produced several booklets on "Preparing Leaders for the 21st Century" and presented ideas to the UCEA Executive Committee. However, in 1984 UCEA leadership decided that the committee was no longer relevant to their scholarly mission. This did not enhance the relationship between school superintendents and was an early indication of a growing gap between academia and school practitioners. According to Maxey (1995) in the past thirty years the professorship has seen a gradual imbalance toward those who "know about" (theory) rather than those who "know how" to do administration.

This imbalance continues to divide the profession in spite of clarion calls for the integration of formal knowledge "knowing about administration" with the best-practice or craft knowledge "knowing how to improve learning and teaching." Art Levine (2005) was on target when he said that the doctoral degree "requires coursework with minimum relevance to practice" (24).

There is great value to the discipline of educational administration for scholarly research—both basic and applied—to increase the depth and value of our knowledge base. This is what scholars are charged to do. However, if researchers in our professional discipline continue failing to notice that we are a professional college with departments, rather than liberal arts or the sciences, they will remain isolated from conversations with front-line school leaders and become albatrosses for schools and students. Therefore, a research-based feedback evaluation system with former students can be the fulcrum to help regain the balance between those who know about and those who know how.

The late Dan Griffiths (1988) warned the profession about the growing gap between professors and school leaders when he wrote, "Departments of educational administration must turn back to schools and establish relationships" (16). Also, Jack Culbertson (1988), NCPEA "Living Legend" said it this way, "Tomorrow's most significant research and training challenges reside primarily in leadership practices and settings of school systems and secondarily in the research and training of professors of educational administration" (1).

Our research finds most research-one programs have not sufficiently attended to Culbertson's warning, and newly minted second tier leadership education professors remain torn between preparing school leaders or preparing articles and papers to meet the demands of tenure and promotion. This delicate balance is maintained by numerous "main line" professors of educational administration, but others remain focused on research agendas that appear removed from the real world of public schools.

Perhaps the rapid infusion of preparation standards into leadership education programs has caused undue tensions between current faculty and accrediting agencies who tend to recreate the One Best Model. This model, based on social systems, leadership styles, and management theories that drive traditional preparation, is in conflict with a new generation of faculty that stresses courses in epistemology, social justice, learning communities, and other less "measurable postmodern curriculum" to prepare a new type of school leader.

Thus, veteran professors are concerned that the field of educational administration is losing its focus on preparing leaders for schools in favor of a postmodern degree focused on social structures and research methods more applicable to education policy or higher education. There can be no better avenue to bring greater unity of purpose in preparing school leaders than asking them what can be done to better prepare them for the complexities the roles of principals and superintendents.

Therefore, we believe that to keep on course the compass must point to former students and their success in improving student performance. Otherwise graduate degrees in leadership education should disappear from the horizon and be replaced with degrees or certificates yet to be discovered.

INTERVIEW QUESTIONS

Graduate programs in educational administration employ various methods in gathering exit information from recent graduates and feedback from graduates established in roles of school leadership. Some faculties gather this important data through face-to-face or online focus groups, online chat rooms, Delphi groups, or face-to-face Nominal Group Techniques. We support any of these methods that will provide ongoing data to assist faculty in conducting annual formative assessments about the effectiveness of the courses, internships, research activities and methods, and faculty. Therefore, the following questions are offered as a means of gathering data from former students now serving in leadership roles.

Questions

These eight questions are field tested and applied in a study of six elite doctoral programs that is discussed below. The questions have proven to be adaptable for master's degree and licensure students as well. We have used the questions to interview former students by phone and face-to-face with successful results (Hoyle & Torres 2008).

1. Since completing your degree (doctorate, master's) what experiences, people, and activities do you recall that have been influential in your success as a building/district school leader?
2. What courses or experiences provided the skills needed for improving school and student performance at the district or school level?
3. What specific courses inside or outside of your major have been helpful or relevant to your success? Provide examples of how specific theories, models, strategies, or methods have helped.
4. What research or methods classes or projects help you today in collecting, tabulating, interpreting, reporting, and distributing data about student, staff, or financial reporting?
5. What words of wisdom, knowledge, interpersonal or communication skills gained in your studies have been important to your success as a campus/district leader?
6. What habits of scholarship (i.e., reading scholarly journals, seeking online research findings, book readings, making speeches, and conducting your own research) are a direct result of your graduate student experiences?
7. What part of your graduate experience could have been more relevant to your work today in school administration? What would you like to see changed in the program?

8. On a scale of 1–5, what is your overall impression of the relevance of your graduate program in shaping your career as a school leader for all students?

1 = Extremely Relevant; 2 = Very Relevant; 3 = Relevant; 4 = Not Very Relevant; and 5 = Not Relevant at All. (Please explain your answers.)

The eight questions can be used as an important step in gathering information about the perceived inadequacies of leadership education programs in public school administration and their graduates. We (Torres & Hoyle 2008) examined former students' perceptions of the overall quality and relevance to actual practice of their respective school leadership preparation programs.

Since Levine (2005) and others tend to paint a broad brush across all doctoral programs in leadership education, we chose to evaluate six of the top ten most prestigious institutions in the United States. These six were among the top ten according to the 2006 *U.S. News and World Report* rankings (*U.S. World and News Report* 2007, 1–14). They are as follows: University of Wisconsin–Madison (1st); Harvard University (3rd), Stanford University (4th), Pennsylvania State University (5th), Ohio State University (6th), and Teachers College, Columbia University (8th).

In addition, each of these programs has been in the top ten for approximately twenty years. No prior studies have assessed top-ranked doctoral programs' ability to prepare successful public school leaders using outcome measures of graduates' reported success. For this reason, the researchers aimed the interviews toward selected graduates of top-ranked programs now serving as leaders of high-performing schools and school districts.

Those selected came from a longer list of graduates provided by program faculty and had been in place for at least three years and produced data confirming high student performance as indicated in "exemplary" or "recognized" state rankings or other awards (i.e., "Blue Ribbon" school or school district). The study was conducted under the assumption that top-ranked doctoral programs are benchmarks for programs of lower rank and that their graduates are better prepared as successful leaders for school improvement.

In addition, research assessing leadership preparation programs have overlooked the perceptions of former doctoral students. Thus, this study assessed whether former students from the six elite institutions perceived that their leadership preparation program played a critical role in their success as school leaders. As indicated previously, the data were gathered through structured telephone interviews.

Responses from thirty former doctoral students were revealing and somewhat similar to several of the experiences of current students. Participating students from all six institutions held the faculty in high esteem and, with few exceptions, agree they chose the program for the national reputation of the faculty and the programs' high ranking. Proximity to the campus was an important factor for some attending Ohio State, Penn State, and Wisconsin.

The seven interview questions asked the former students to reflect on their performance as school leaders and the impact of their doctoral experiences on their success. Two questions, #1, and #5, focused on human interpersonal dimensions of their graduate school experiences while questions #2 and #3 asked them to judge the value of their theoretical or methodological courses for their current leadership responsibilities. Next, they were asked (#6) if they were currently engaged in habits of scholarship, and question #7 invited them to identify weaknesses or suggest changes that were needed to improve or update the course work and assignments.

Finally, the graduates were asked to sum up using a five-point scale their overall sense of the relevance of their entire doctoral experience to their daily tasks in leading schools and school districts.

The responses to the first question set the stage for the other five since it sought to capture the big picture of their doctoral experience and its influence on their current leadership effectiveness. Five themes emerged from the interviews of students from the six programs. Students found an "intellectually stimulating" environment created by "highly skilled faculty" that inspired their success as school leaders.

Their professors provided outstanding guidance during their dissertations and became "role models" who instilled "norms of excellence" and "rich interactions" with other students and faculty throughout their degree program. While these outstanding graduates found the course work to be "tough" others found that the cohort model created a very supportive and diverse learning community. Students from four programs expressed the expert way that faculty taught them how to link theory to practice in schools.

One student remarked that "professors taught the theories I use every day in decision making and leadership" (Hoyle & Torres 2008, 226). Some former students from four institutions reported that both critical consumption of research and engagement in scholarly activities led them to copresent papers at conferences. While graduates' perceptions were overall very positive about their experiences, they did offer a few caveats about the programs. The saw obvious disconnects between the programs and state licensure and regretted the fading relationship between faculty, course content, and the real world of schools and school administration.

Students at three institutions questioned the applicability of course work to practice and commented on the "big name" faculty retiring. Stanford and Wisconsin graduates commented on the retirement of faculty "stars" in recent years. All of the retirees were former school principals or superintendents who also distinguished themselves as scholars in educational administration.

It was obvious to the researchers that several younger faculty replacements had very little if any public school administrative experience and most current students were not preparing to be school leaders, but university researchers or policy analysts. Two former students commented that they had professors with no practical base upon which to teach, a troubling trend discussed previously.

Overall the graduates' assessment was very positive. They gave high marks for their programs, generating an overall mean of 1.1 (i.e., a score of 1 being extremely relevant and 5 being not relevant at all). Only a slight difference appeared between the ratings of former students from public and private programs.

The purpose of this study was to seek answers for closing the gap in the research literature tying doctoral programs' preparation of school administrators to their results as school leaders. While the former students viewed their doctoral experiences as very relevant to their roles in creating successful schools and school districts for students, they are concerned about the changes in programs since they graduated. They expressed concern that some faculty had little or no public school experience and fewer contacts with school superintendents, principals, and state policy makers.

While the findings from this study were not meant to be representative of the experiences of the general former student population who earned doctorates in leadership, valuable insights were gained. Greater efforts must be made to maintain high quality graduate programs for full-time and part-time students. The new models (e.g., online, weekend, summers and off-campus sites) offer more streamlined ways to earn degrees in educational administration.

Professors must work to narrow the quality gaps within programs to assure that our current and future graduates who lead schools and school districts gain more than a diploma earned online or on campus. As found in the study of six elite programs, gaps are growing between those who teach administration and those who administer schools. Greater collaboration must occur among university programs in education and professional administrator organizations to recruit the best and most culturally responsive leaders for careers in public education. Thus, we offer the above questions as a guide and as a first step in assessing the impact of graduate programs on the leadership effectiveness of our graduates.

In addition to the open-ended questionnaire, we offer the validated forced-choice questionnaire (table 7.1) to gather feedback from graduates or current students enrolled in a PSM cohort program (Hoyle & Oates 2000).

This forced-choice questionnaire could be enhanced by asking the respondents to explain their answers on each item in order to gain more information. Perhaps the primary reason for surveying graduates goes far beyond the feedback value for program improvement. The survey data is a vital piece of information to keep our programs relevant, but the most important reason we improve our programs is to prepare principals and superintendents who educate children and youth for successful and fulfilling lives.

Table 7.1. Doctoral Cohort Questionnaire

Please respond to the Doctoral Cohort Questionnaire (DCQ) items by circling SA, Strongly Agree; A, Agree; D, Disagree; or SD, Strongly Disagree.

Item No.	*SA*	*A*	*D*	*SD*
1. The most difficult element of the admissions criteria was the presentation portion in the interview.	SA	A	D	SD
2. The written exercise was the most difficult element of the admissions criteria.	SA	A	D	SD
3. The course of study met or is meeting my professional expectations to prepare me for the next level of my career.	SA	A	D	SD
4. The sequence in the course offerings was/is appropriate with out too much overlap in the content.	SA	A	D	SD
5. The course of study balances theory with practice.	SA	A	D	SD
6. The course of study places appropriate emphasis on curriculum and instruction.	SA	A	D	SD
7. The course of study includes appropriate numbers of tools courses (i.e., evaluation statistics, tests and measurement, and research).	SA	A	D	SD
8. The summer courses are as convenient as possible to meet the demands of your job.	SA	A	D	SD
9. The weekend courses are as convenient as possible to meet the demand of your job.	SA	A	D	SD
10. The superintendent and board was/is supportive of your efforts to complete the degree.	SA	A	D	SD
11. The coursework in educational technology was adequate to meet your needs.	SA	A	D	SD
12. The cohort members usually bonded and assisted each other in the learning process.	SA	A	D	SD
13. Your mentor/advisor was usually available when you needed him or her.	SA	A	D	SD
14. You were adequately prepared for the written and oral comprehensive/preliminary exams.	SA	A	D	SD
15. You were given ample assistance in identifying a research topic for your dissertation.	SA	A	D	SD

8

Final Words

Is this book the last word in preparing exemplary principals and superintendents? We have attempted to make suggestions based on a combined sixty years in education and forty-seven years teaching and advising students in educational administration. We believe we have touched the bases in the right order, and, if you will revisit them, you will perhaps avoid some pitfalls and find best practices in program planning, faculty team work, and student advisement.

We hope we have created a book that responds to much of the criticism of leadership education by including research and best practices that have inspired positive improvements in preparation programs and in the graduates leading successful schools and school districts. Also perhaps we have produced helpful ideas and strategies to assist our colleagues who are never totally satisfied with the quality of their leadership education programs. We challenge our colleagues to produce the kinds of school leaders our children deserve and a historical context of our discipline or professional field since the turn of the twentieth century.

We recorded some of the strongest winds of change that invigorated early school and classroom management techniques and inspired today's search for quality systems and issues about equity, justice, and accountability. The One Best Model labeled by William Boyd and Bruce Cooper in 1987 has never gone away and is reinforced by the standards movement that began with the 1983 breezy "*Guidelines*" and evolved into hurricane force *ISLLC 2008 Leadership Policy Standards and Functions.*

This national movement is based on the belief that school leaders who possess these minimum standards and related functions will have the cognitive structures necessary for gaining deeper understanding of school administration and leadership. While this One Best Model does not go unchallenged by pundits and practicing school administrators, it does have a strong foothold since it is supported by chief state school officers and professional administrator associations.

Therefore, rather than challenge this national trend for master's degree program accreditations and licensure, we have created *Six Steps to Preparing Exemplary Principals and Superintendents*: 1. Selecting the best and brightest students; 2. Pretesting entering master's and doctoral students; 3. Aligning master's degree programs with the *2008 ISSLC Educational Leadership Policy Standards*, and doctoral programs with the canons of research and best practices; 4. Creating and maintaining effective student advisory committees; 5. Creating and maintaining effective office support staff; and 6. Conducting annual program reviews with graduates serving as principals or superintendents.

Thus, we bring our experience and related literature to the best practices of attracting servant-oriented master's and doctoral students, diagnosing their entry-level knowledge and providing the best committee and other support to help assure their success in graduate school and as leaders of successful schools and school systems. We offer our colleagues the LSI as a rather simple way to assess entering master's degree students' knowledge and participation levels in the thirty-one functions.

We follow this assessment with a step-by-step process to assist in guiding each student to mastery of the thirty-one functions and provide directed readings, course suggestions, and student projects. These suggestions will help beginning master's degree students reach higher levels of cognition and guide them toward more reflective, servant-driven leadership styles. Also, we created six higher cognition questions around social, leadership, and education issues to assist faculty in assessing the writing and skill level of entry-level doctoral students. To avoid some of the problems faculty and students face in creating graduate committees, we provide advice on ways to create committees for master's and doctoral students.

Our experience tells us that this committee must be compatible, knowledgeable, but primarily interested in helping the student increase in "knowledge and wisdom" and help reduce interpersonal conflicts that can occur within the committee. We extol the value of hiring and maintaining talented office staff, especially the academic advisors who literally hold the hand and guide most beginning students through the maze of graduate studies and provide the logistics to keep the department or program running smoothly.

The office personnel are usually the first contact for new students and can have a profound influence on the student deciding to enter and complete the master's or doctoral degree. Finally, we agree that one of the glaring gaps in our discipline is the sparse feedback from former students now serving as school administrators. Are we teaching the right concepts and offering the best field-based experiences that directly affect our graduates' abilities in leading high-performing and student-centered schools and school systems?

We hope our former student assessment questionnaire and the Doctoral Cohort Questionnaire (see table 7.1) will assist you in beginning or improving your annual assessment of your former students. We will find much professional fulfillment in completing this book if our colleagues gain ideas on ways to improve their intellectual and interpersonal impact on our graduates and their students in public and private schools. Our rewards will come when our graduates create schools and school systems that help assure that all students find success in life.

Appendix A

Dissertation Criteria

DISSERTATION EVALUATION CRITERIA

This evaluation criteria form has proven to be very helpful to us in conducting external reviews of doctoral programs and advising colleagues with the dissertation process.

Dissertation/Record of Study Title:
Student:
Advisory Committee Members:
Rating Scale: Ten Points (10) = Highest Score; One Point (1) = Lowest Score

1. Theoretical Framework: Depth and quality of research literature. ____________
2. Problem Statement: Level of specificity of the research problem linked to the theoretical framework. ____________
3. Purpose of Study: Clarity of the statement and its link to the problem statement. ____________
4. Research Procedures: Degree of specificity in identifying the population/sample/subjects and the steps/methods required in data collection. ____________
5. Research Methodologies: Clarity and comprehension of the research method or methods (quantitative/qualitative/or mixed) required to precisely analyze the data. ____________

6. Research Findings/Analysis: These are displayed according to the research objectives/question/hypotheses and clarity of the narrative and tables. ____________
7. Conclusions: Are the conclusion statements linked closely to the findings and the theory base of the study (i.e., does the study add to or challenge the theoretical framework)? ____________
8. References: Are the references selected from the most relevant research around the research problem, purpose, and objectives? ______

Average score _______
Comments by the reviewer:

Appendix B

Model Programs

Table B.1. Model Degree Programs

Model Master's Degree Plan #1: Trinity University, San Antonio, Texas, Program Overview	
Fall 1: 6 hours	
EDUC 5390	Educational Administration and Organization
EDUC 5391	The School Management Function
Spring 1: 9 hours	
EDUC 5392	Administration of the Elementary and Secondary School
EDUC 5393	Research Methods
EDUC 5394	Supervised Practicum
Summer 1: 6 hours	
EDUC 5395	Curriculum Development
EDUC 6396	Problems in Administration
Fall II: 6 hours	
EDUC 6390	School Law and Finance
EDUC 6391	Advanced Problems in Administration
Spring II: 9 hours	
EDUC 5387	Independent Study: Problems in Practice
EDUC 6693	Internship

Graduation Portfolio: Students are required to submit a graduation portfolio that provides compelling evidence that they have met NCATE standards, Texas licensing standards, and Trinity University standards.

Table B.2 Model Degree Program

Model Master's Degree Plan #2: Texas A&M University Master Calendar for M.Ed. Program (No Summer)

Year	*Summer Semester*	*Fall Semester*	*Spring Semester*
Year one	Summer reading list	EDAD 603 Foundation of Education	EDAD 609 Public School Law
		EDAD 604 Culturally Responsive Leadership	EDAD Change in Educational Organizations
		EDAD 605 Elementary & Secondary Principalship	EDAD Organizational Learning
Year two	1. Field-based contacts with mentors in each student's home district	EDAD 608 School Finance	EDAD Instructional Leadership Development
	2. Field/clinical requirements embedded in all courses	EDAD 622 Quality Educational Systems	EDAD Developing School Community Partnerships
	3. Students prepare a comprehensive portfolio linking coursework to field projects	EDAD 635 Administration of Special Services	EDAD Proseminar applied data (techniques)

Notes:
1. Admission: 12–14 students
2. Courses: 5 Saturday Combination
3. Class Time: 6–8 hours per meeting
4. Web Enhancement: 1–3 hours per week
5. Require Students to Attend TASSP/TEPSA Summer and Fall Conferences
6. Total: 36-hour Program
7. Present Portfolio in spring semester that serves as evidence the student can meet NCATE
8. Present Portfolio in spring semester that serves as evidence the student can meet Texas Licensure Standards and Texas A&M University Program Standards
9. Friday Night Lecture Series by Faculty or Guests

MODEL DEGREE PLAN #3: UNIVERSITY OF WISCONSIN–MADISON

University of Wisconsin–Madison, Department of Educational Leadership and Policy Analysis

Ph.D. Program

For greater detail on each required and elective course see www.education.wisc.edu/elpa/.

Overall, doctoral students must take seventy-five credits of course work across the categories as described. Courses may only be counted in one category. At least thirty-nine credits of the total program have to be in

Table B.3. Model Degree Program

Model Doctoral Degree Plan #3: The University of Wisconsin–Madison Program Overview

Course Requirements	*Credits*
Introduction to the Field	6
Core Knowledge	12
Program Depth	9
Electives	15
Minor	12
Research Methods and Design	12
Research/ Dissertation	9
TOTAL	75

Educational Leadership and Policy Analysis Courses. Transfer students from other institutions must enroll for at least thirty-nine credits from University of Wisconsin–Madison; no more than six credits of special student work are applicable toward degree requirements.

I. Introduction to the Field (6 credits)
These introductory courses lay the foundation framework for work in the department. Students are strongly encouraged to take the introduction to the field at the beginning of their studies.

ELPA 701 Introduction to Elementary and Secondary Education Administration
ELPA 701 Introduction to Higher and Post-Secondary Education

II. Core Knowledge (12 credits)
The department believes that students in educational administration should be familiar with four program areas of knowledge. Organizations and Planning; Program and Instructional Leadership and Management; Politics, Policy, and Finance; and Learning and Diversity. Knowledge in each of these areas is focused on providing a theoretical theory and empirical research knowledge base to facilitate improvements in teaching and learning in educational organizations. Therefore the department requires that students take one listed course in each of the four program areas (12 credits total).

III. Program Depth (9 credits)
The department believes that the students should take at least one of the four program areas. Therefore, each student will take at least three

additional courses in one of the four program areas: Organizations and Planning; Program and Instructional Leadership and Management; Politics, Policy, and Finance; and Learning and Diversity. At least one of the three additional courses must be in Educational Administration.

IV. Electives (15 credits)
Students may take five courses inside or outside of the department to provide depth or breadth to program focus.

IV. Minor/Supporting Coursework (12 credits)
The minor is a rational, unified set of courses taken outside of the department that have a clearly articulated theme or focus which allows the student to develop knowledge in a related area of study.

V. Research Methods and Design (12 credits)
Students must complete a sequence of courses in research methods and design, focusing on either quantitative or qualitative methods. Students choosing to focus on quantitative methods should take two statistical methods courses and one qualitative methods course. Students choosing to focus on qualitative methods should take two qualitative methods courses and one statistical methods course. After the methods requirement has been met, all students should take the research design course.

VI. Research/Thesis (9 credits)
Students may enroll for up to a maximum of nine credits of research/thesis and or independent reading.

MODEL DOCTORAL DEGREE PLAN-EXECUTIVE ED.D. PROGRAM FROM SETON HALL UNIVERSITY

The Seton Hall University Executive Ed.D. program is in its twelfth year of operation. Over three hundred students have enrolled in this "fast track doctoral" program, and it has produced over two hundred graduates. All applicants for the Executive Ed.D. program must serve in a K–12 campus or school district as a practicing administrator to be considered for the program. This maturation is reflected in high admissions scores (average MAT/GRE scores in 80th percentile and a 60 percent acceptance rate of applicants) which include points for success in leading schools to high performance, publications, and community involvement. In most cases applicants for the executive program tend to be self-motivated personalities and are on a fast track to complete the doctorate in two to three years. Students invest considerable time and resources on campus in coursework and research, interacting online and by telephone with professors and fellow cohort members who share similar motivation to complete degree requirements as promptly as possible. The classes are conducted on ten weekends and two summer sessions over a two-year period. Thirty students are admitted to each cohort with an upfront expense of approximately $60,000 that covers everything but travel and hotel expenses over a two-year period. The program staff strives to remove obstacles to assist the student by being available every day. Registration for the block of courses common to all students and books and guides are given to students each year of the program. One hundred meals are arranged, as well as banquets, receptions, barbeques, lectures, and dinner-theater events to give balance to the academic program and to bond students to each other.

Executive Ed.D. Degree Plan

The degree modules include 90 credits of which 45 must be taken at Seton Hall University. The core (15) credits include two courses in statistics and one or two courses in qualitative methods and survey research methods, organizational structures, curriculum, research design and organization, school law, and educational finance/business management. Three credits are required in Foundations/Interdisciplinary studies. The students must pass a qualifying exam based on the five core courses and a comprehensive exam that included statistics and research and three of the other domains. Also the students may choose the option to examine a contemporary problem and attempt to solve the problem using problem analysis or conduct a comprehensive field based survey of an actual school system. If students master the qualifying exam, they are declared candidates for the degree. Since the students are encouraged to complete their dissertation proposals during their first semester, they can complete the intensive, accelerated program in two years.

According to a 2008 External Review Report, the Seton Hall fast track program has become a major player by offering full-time campus and systems-level administrators the opportunity to complete their degree without returning to campus for full-time residency. Graduates are fiercely loyal to the program, which has resulted in the recruitment of several students by program graduates who continually promote Seton Hall University and the effect that their graduate experiences had on their professional and personal lives. The 2008 External Report concluded that the "Executive Ed.D. model" has become well recognized across the country and has influenced other leadership education doctoral program faculty to consider similar adjustments to their programs to not only maintain high quality but also accommodate the busy work schedules of experienced school leaders.

For more information about this program contact the Office of the Dean, College of Education and Human Services, 400 South Orange Ave., South Orange, N.J. 07079 or www.shu.edu.

References

Achilles, C. (1999). *Let's put kids first, finally getting class size right.* Thousand Oaks, Calif.: Corwin Press.

———. (2005). *A sense of history might help!* Paper presented at the National Conference of professors of educational administration, Washington, D.C.

———. (2009). Front-line education administration (EDAD) requires concepts of schooling outcomes beyond test scores. In C. Achilles, B. Irby, B. Alford, & G. Perreault (Eds.), Remember our mission: Making education and schools better for students (71–83). *The 2009 Yearbook of the National Council of Professors of Educational Administration,* Lancaster, Pa.: DEStech Publications, Inc.

Arthur, W. (2007). Personal conversation.

Arthur, W., & Benjamin, L. (1999). Psychology applied to business. In A. Stec & D. Bernstein (Eds.), *Psychology: Fields and application* (98–270). Boston: Houghton-Mifflin.

Badgett, J., & Christmann, E. (2009a). *Designing elementary instruction and assessment: Using the cognitive domain.* Thousand Oaks, Calif.: Corwin Press.

Badgett, J., & Christmann, E. (2009b). *Designing middle and high school instruction and assessment.* Thousand Oaks, Calif.: Corwin Press.

Baker, B. (2009). Within-district resource allocation and the marginal costs of providing equal opportunity: Evidence from Texas and Ohio. *Education Policy Analysis Archives,* 17(3), 1–28.

Barnett, K., & McCormich, J. (2004). Leadership and individual principal-teacher relationships in schools. *Educational Administration Quarterly,* 40(3), 406–434.

Beaudoin, M., & Taylor, M. (2009). *Responding to the culture of bullying and disrespect.* Thousand Oaks, Calif.: Corwin Press.

Berliner, D. (1988). Simple views of effective teaching and simple theory of classroom instruction. In D. Berliner & B. Rosenshine (Eds.), *Talks to teachers* (93–110). New York: Random House.

Bingham, W., & Jones, T. (2008). School district and financial operations. In J. Vornberg (Ed.), *Texas public school organization and administration* (395–411). Dubuque, Iowa: Kendall Hunt.

Bjork, L. G., & Ginsberg, R. (1995). Principles of reform and reforming principal training: A theoretical perspective. *Educational Administration Quarterly*, 31(1), 11–37.

Bloom, B. (1982). *All our children's learning*. New York: McGraw-Hill.

Bottoms, G., & O'Neill, K. (2001). *Preparing a new breed of school principals: It's time for action*. Atlanta: Southern Regional Education Board.

Brown, K., Anfara, V., and Roney, K. (2004). Student achievement in high performing middle schools and low performing urban middle schools. *Education and Urban Society*, 36(4), 428–456.

Brown, K. M. (2004). Leadership for social justice and equity: Weaving a transformative framework and pedagogy. *Educational Administration Quarterly*, 40(1), 77–108.

Brubaker, D. (2006). *The charismatic leader*. Thousand Oaks, Calif.: Corwin Press.

Byrd, J., & Drews, C. (2008). The relationship between resource allocation and student achievement. *School Leadership Review*, 3(2), 35–65.

Campbell, R., & Gregg, R. (Eds.). (1957). *Administrative behavior in education*. New York; Harper & Brothers Publishers.

Cicchelli, T., Marcus, S., & Weiner, M. (2002). Superintendents' dialog in a professional Development model. *Education and Urban Society*, 29(3), 317–341.

Cohen, D. K., Moffitt, S. L., & Goldin, S. (2007). Policy and practice: The dilemma. *American Journal of Education*, 113(4), 515–548.

Cooper, B., & Boyd, W. (1987). The evolution of training for school administrators. In J. Murphy & P. Hallinger (Eds.), *Approaches to administrative training in education*. New York: State University of New York Press.

Corcoran, T., & Goertz, M. (2005). The governance of public education. In S. Furman & M. Lazerson (Eds.), *The public schools* (25–57). Philadelphia: The Annenberg Foundation.

Cornish, E. (2004). *Futuring: The exploration of the future*. Bethesda, Md.: World Future Society.

Creighton, T. (2001). *Schools and data*. Thousand Oaks, Calif.: Corwin Press.

———. (2006). *The educators guide for using data to improve decision making*. Thousand Oaks, Calif.: Corwin Press.

Creighton, T., Lunenburg, F., Irby, B., & Nie, Y. (2004). *Educational administration director*, (22nd ed.). Huntsville, TX: National Council of Professors of Educational Administration.

Cruickshank, D., & Haefele, D. (2001). Good teachers, plural. *Educational Leadership*, 58(5), 26–30.

Cuban, L. (2001, January). Why bad reforms won't give us good schools. *The American Prospect*, 12(1), 303–312.

Cubberly, E. P. (1927). *State school administration*. Boston: Houghton-Mifflin.

Culbertson, J. (1983). Theory in educational administration: Echoes for critical thinkers. *Educational Researcher*, 12(10), 15–22.

———. (1988). A century's quest for a knowledge base. In N. Boyan (Ed.), *Handbook of research on educational administration* (3–26). New York: Longman.

Cunningham, B., & Cordeiro, P. (2000). *Educational administration: A problem based approach*. Boston: Allyn & Bacon.

———. (2003). *Educational leadership. A problem-based approach*. Boston: Allyn & Bacon.

———. (2006). *Educational leadership*, (3rd ed.). Boston: Pearson.

Danitz, T. (2009). States confronting school superintendent shortage. *Stateline.org, Pew Center on the States*, www.stateline.org.

Dantley, M. (2003). Purpose driven leadership: The spiritual imperative in guiding schools beyond high-stakes testing and minimum proficiency *Education and Urban Society*, 35(23), 273–291.

Darling-Hammond, L., et al. (2007). *Preparing leadership for a changing world: Lessons from exemplary leadership development programs*. New York: Wallace Foundation Press.

Devita, C. (2007). *Wallace Report on Principals*. Washington, D.C.: Wallace Foundation.

Dimmock, C., & Walker, A. (2000). Globalization and societal culture: Redefining schooling and school leadership in the twenty first century. *Compare: A Journal of Comparative Education*, 30(3), 303–312.

Dunklee, D., & Shoop, R. (2001). *The principal's quick reference guide to school law: Reducing liability, litigation, and other potential legal tangles*. Thousand Oaks, Calif.: Corwin Press.

Educational leadership policy standards (2008). Washington, D.C.: Council of Chief States School Officers.

Elmore, D. (1996). Getting to scale with successful educational practices. In S. H. Furman & J. A. O'Day (Eds.), *Rewards and reforms: Creating educational Incentives that work up* (294–329). San Francisco: Jossey-Bass.

Elmore, R. (2007). Breaking the cartel. *Phi Delta Kappan*, 88(7), 517–518.

English, F. (2006). The unintended consequences of a standardized knowledge base in educational leadership preparation. *Educational Administration Quarterly*, 42(3), 461–472.

Epstein, J. L. (1995). School/family/community partnerships: Caring for the children we share. *Phi Delta Kappan*, 76(9), 701–712.

Everson, S. T. (2009). A professional doctorate in educational leadership: Saint Louis University's Ed.D. program. *Peabody Journal of Education*, 84(1), 86–99.

Flanary, D. (2009). Description of the web-based NASSP leadership skills assessment program. Reston, Va.: National Association of Secondary School Principals.

Foster, W. (1986). *Paradigms and promises: New approaches to educational Administration*. Amherst, N.Y.: Prometheus Books.

Furman, S., & Lazerson, M. (Eds.). (2005). *The public schools*. Philadelphia: University of Pennsylvania Press.

Glasman, N., Cibulka, J., & Ashby, D. (2002). Program self-evaluation for continuous Improvement. *Educational Administration Quarterly*, 38(2), 257–288.

Glass, T., Bjork, L., & Brunner, C. (2000). *The 2000 study of the superintendency: A look at the superintendent in the time of reform*. Arlington, Va.: The American Association of School Administrators.

Glickman, C., Gordon, S., & Gordon, J. M (2010). *Supervision and instructional leadership*, (8th ed.). Boston: Allyn & Bacon.

Goddard, R. (2003). Relational networks, social trust, and norms. A social capital perspective on students' chances of academic success. *Educational Evaluation and Policy Analysis*, 62(1), 59–74.

Goddard, R., & LoGerfo, L. (2007). Measuring emergent organizational properties: A comparison of the predictive validity and intergroup variability of self vs group referent perceptions. *Educational and Psychological Measurement*, 65(5), 845–858.

Goddard, R., & Skrla, L. (2006). The influence of school social context on teachers's collective efficacy beliefs. *Educational Administration Quarterly*, 42(2), 216–235.

Good, T., & Brophy, J (1997) *Looking into classrooms* (7th ed.). New York: Addison & Wesley.

Goodlad, J. (1984). *A place called school: Prospects for the future*. New York: McGraw-Hill.

Gootman, E., & Gebeloff, R. (2009). *Principals younger and freer, but raise doubts in the schools*. Inside NYTimes.com, 1–2.

Graham, B. (2007). Assessing educational leadership preparation framework. In L. Lemasters & F. Papa (Eds.), At the tipping point: Navigating the course for the preparation of educational administrators. *The 2007 Yearbook of the National Council of Professors of Educational Administration* (40–49). Lancaster, Pa.: DEStech Publications, Inc.

Green, R. (2010). *The four dimensions of principal leadership*. Boston: Allyn & Bacon.

Greenfield, T. (1975). Theory about organization: A new perspective and its implications for schools. In M. Hughes (Ed.), *Administering education: International challenge* (71–99). London, Athlone Publishers.

Griffiths, D. (1956). *Human relations in school administration*. New York: Longman, Inc.

———. (Ed.). (1964). *Behavioral science and educational administration*. Chicago: The University of Chicago Press.

Griffiths, D., Stout, R., & Forsyth, P. (Eds.). (1988). *Leaders for America's schools*. Berkeley: McCutchan Publishers.

Grogan, M., & Andrews, R. (2002). Defining preparation and professional development for the future. *Educational Administration Quarterly*, 38(2): 233–256.

Guterman, J. (2009). Where have all the principals gone: The acute school-leader shortage. *www.edutopia.org/principal-shortage?page*.

Guthrie, J., & Schuermann, P. (2010). *Successful school leadership: Planning, politics, performance, and power*. Boston: Allyn & Bacon.

Guthrie, J., Springer, M., Rolle, R., & Houch, E. A. (2007). *Modern educational finance and policy*. Boston: Allyn & Bacon.

Hale, E., & Moorman, H. (2003). *Preparing school principals: A national perspective on policy and program innovations*. Washington, D.C. Institute of Educational Leadership and Edwardsville: Illinois Education Research Council.

Hallinger, P. and Snidvongs, K. (2008). Educating leaders: Is there anything to learn from business management? *Educational Management Administration and Leadership*, 36(1), 9–31.

Hargreaves, A., & Fullan, M. (1998). *What's worth fighting for out there?* New York: Teachers College Press.

Harris, S. (2006). *Best practices of award winning secondary school principals*. Thousand Oaks, Calif.: Corwin Press.

Harris, S., Moore, H., & Farrow, V. (2008). Extending transfer of learning theory to transformative learning theory: A model for promoting teacher leadership. *Theory into Practice,* 47(4), 318–327.

Henderson, J. (1995). Personal conversation about Duquesne's doctoral program.

Hill, P. T., & Celio, M. B. (1998). *Fixing urban schools.* Washington D.C.: Brookings.

Houston, P., & Sokolow, S. (2006). *The spiritual dimension of leadership.* Thousand Oaks, Calif.: Corwin Press.

Hoy, A., & Hoy, W., (2006). *Instructional leadership: A research based guide to learning in schools.* Boston: Pearson.

Hoy, W., & Miskel, C. (1991). *Educational administration.* Boston: McGraw-Hill.

———. (2008). *Educational administration* (8th ed.). Boston: McGraw-Hill.

Hoy, W., & Tarter, J. (1995). *Administrators solving the problems of practice: Decision making, concepts, cases, and consequences.* Boston: Allyn & Bacon.

Hoyle, J. (1983). *Guidelines for the preparation of school administrators.* Arlington, Va.: American Association of School Administrators.

———. (1991). Educational administration has a knowledge base. *Record in Educational Administration and Supervision,* 12(1), 21–27.

———. (1993). *Professional standards for the superintendency.* Lanham, Md.: Rowman & Littlefield Education

———. (2002). *Leadership and the force of love: Six keys to motivating with love.* Thousand Oaks, Calif.: Corwin Press.

———. (2005, August). The standards movement in educational administration: The quest for respect. In T. Creighton, S. Harris, & J. Coleman (Eds.), *Crediting the past challenging the present, creating the future* (23–42). National Conference of Professors of educational administration. Research report presented August 2005 in Washington, D.C.

———. (2007a). A preparation mystery: Why some succeed and others fail. *Planning and Changing,* 38(3&4), 148–164

———. (2007b, Spring). Educational leadership preparation programs lacking in quality? Bunk? *School Leadership News.* American education research association, AERA division A. 3–4.

———. (2007c). *Leadership and futuring: Making visions happen.* Thousand Oaks, Calif.: Corwin Press.

———. (2009). The educational leader: Diplomat and communicator for all students. In P. Houston, P. Blankenship, & R. Cole (Eds.). *Leaders as communicators and diplomats* (25–45). Thousand Oaks, Calif.: Corwin Press.

Hoyle, J., Bjork, L., Collier, V., & Glass, T. (2005). *The superintendent as CEO: Standards-based performance.* Thousand Oaks, Calif.: Corwin Press.

Hoyle, J., & Crenshaw, H. (1996). *Interpersonal sensitivity.* Larchmont, N.Y.: Eye on Education.

Hoyle, J., English, F., & Steffy, F. (1985). *Skills for successful school leaders.* Arlington, Va.: The American Association of School Administrators.

———. (1998). *Skills for successful 21st century school leaders.* Lanham, Md.: Rowman & Littlefield Education.

Hoyle, J., & Oates, A. (2000). The professional studies model (psm) and professional development for practicing administrators in the new millennium. In P. Jenlink & M. Jenlink (Eds.), *Marching into a new millennium: Challenges to educational leadership* (104–116). The Eighth Yearbook of the National Council of Professors of Educational Administration. Lanham, Md.: The Scarecrow Press.

Hoyle, J., & Torres, M. (2006). Six steps to preparing exemplary principals and superintendents. Paper presented at the National Conference of Professors of Educational Administration, San Diego, Calif.: August 2006.

Hoyle, J., & Torres, M. (2008). Exploring the link between school leadership preparation and practice: An analysis of former students' impressions on the relevance of their doctoral experience at six elite institutions. *Planning and Changing*, 39(3&4), 213–39.

Irby, Brown & Yang (2009). The synergistic leadership theory: A 21st century leadership theory. In C. Achilles, et al. (Eds.), *Remember our mission: Making education and schools better for students*, 16th Annual NCPEA Yearbook. Lancaster, Pa.: Destech Publications, 93–109.

ISLLC/NCATE *Standards for advanced programs in educational leadership* (2008). Washington, D.C.: The Council of Chief State School Officers.

Jackson, B., & Kelly, C. (2002). Exceptional and innovative programs in educational leadership. *Educational Administration Quarterly*, 38(2), 192–212.

Jahangiri, L., Mucciolo, T., and Spielman, A. (2008). Assessment of teaching effectiveness in U.S. Dental schools and the value of triangulation. *Journal of Dental Education*, 72(6), 707–718.

Jazzar, M., & Algozzine, B. (2007). *Keys to successful 21st century educational leadership*. Boston: Pearson.

Jenlink, P., & Jenlink, K. (2008). Creating democratic learning communities: Transformative work as spatial practice. *Theory into Practice*, 47(4), 311–317.

Knapp, M. (2002). *Understanding how policy meets practice* (Occasional Paper). Seattle: Center for the Study of Teaching and Policy.

Koschoreck, J. (2001). Accountability and educational equity in the transformation of an urban district. *Education and Urban Society*, 33(3), 284–304.

Lachmann, L. M., & Taylor, L. (1995). *Schools for all: Educating children in a diverse society*. Albany: Delmar Publishers.

Lee, V. E., & Smith, J. B. (1999). Social support and achievement in Chicago: The role of school academic press. *American Educational Research Journal*, 36(4), 907–945.

Leithwood, K. (2007). *Successful school principalship in times of change: An international perspective*. Dordrecht, the Netherlands: Springer.

Leithwood, K., & Levin, B. (2005). Assessing leadership effects on student learning. In W. Hoy and C. Miskel (Eds.), *Contemporary issues in educational policy and school outcomes* (53–76). Greenwich, Conn.: Information Age.

Leithwood, K. A., & Steinbach, R. (1992). Improving the problem-solving expertise of school administrators: Theory and practice. *Education and Urban Society*, 24(3), 317–345.

Levine, A. (2005). *Educating school leaders*. Washington, D.C.: The Education Schools Project.

Lincoln, Y., & Guba, E. (1985). *Naturalistic inquiry*. Thousand Oaks, Calif.: Sage.

Lunnenburg, F. (2002). Improving student achievement: Some structural incompatibilities. In G. Perreault & Lunnenburg, F. (Eds.), *The changing world of school administration* (1–30). Lanham, Md.: Scarecrow Press.

Lunnenburg, F., & Ornstein, A. (2003). *Educational administration* (4th ed.). Belmont, Calif.: Wadsworth.

Marshall, C., & Oliva, M. (2010). *Leadership for social justice* (2nd ed.). Boston: Allyn & Bacon.

Marzano, R., Waters, T., & McNulty, B. (2005). *School leadership that works: From research to results.* Alexandria, Va.: Association for Supervision and Curriculum Development.

Maxey, S. J. (1995). *Democracy, chaos, and new school order.* Thousand Oaks, CA: Corwin Press.

McCarthy, M. (1999). How are school leaders prepared? Trends and future directions. *Educational Horizons*, 77(2), 78–81.

McCarthy, M., & Kuh, F. (1997). *Continuity and change: The educational leadership professoriate.* Columbia, MO: The University Council for Educational Administration.

McLeod, J. et al. (2003). *The key elements of classroom management: Managing time and space, student behavior, and instructional strategies.* Alexandria, Va.: ASCD.

McNeil, J. (1996). *Curriculum: A comprehensive introduction.* Los Angeles: Harper Collins.

Meyer, J. W. (1986). Organizational factors affecting legislation in education. In D. L. Kirp & D. N. Jensen (Eds), *School days, rule days: The legislation regulation of education.* Philadelphia: Falmer, 256–277.

Meyer, J., & Rowan, B. (1983). Formal structure as myth and ceremony. *Journal of sociology*, 83, 340-363.

Mitchell, C., & McSpadden, L. (1977). An examination of admissions criteria for Graduate students in departments of educational administration. *UCEA Review* 18(3), 20-25.

Murphy, J. (1990). Principal instructional leadership. In L. Lotto & P. Thurston (Eds.), *Advances in educational administration: Changing perspective on the school*, 163–200.

———. (2006). Dancing lessons for elephants: Reforming ed school leadership programs. *Phi Delta Kappan*, 87(7), 489–491.

———. (2007). Questioning the core of university-based programs for preparing school leaders. *Phi Delta Kappan*, 88(8), 582–586.

Murphy, J., & Hallinger, P. (1987). *Approaches to administrative training in education.* New York: SUNY Press.

Murphy, J., Moorman, H., & McCarthy, M. (2008). A framework for rebuilding initial certification and preparation programs in educational leadership: Lessons from whole-state reform initiatives. *Teachers College Record*, 110(10), 2172–2203.

Murphy, J., & Vriesenga, M. (2005). *Research on preparation programs in educational administration: An analysis.* UCEA monograph series. Columbia: University Council for Educational administration, University of Missouri.

———. (2006). Research on school leadership preparation in the United States: An analysis. *School Leadership and Management*, 26(2), 183–195.

NASSP Assessment Center. (2008). *Web-based NASSP leadership skills assessment program.* Reston, VA: National Association of Secondary School Principals.

Nathan, B., & Cascio, W. (1986). Technical and legal standards. In R. A. Beck (Ed.), *Performance assessment: Methods and applications*. Baltimore, MD: Johns Hopkins Press, 1–50.

National Center for Education Statistics. (n.d.). nces.edu.gov/fastfacts/display.Asp?id=65.

Newman F., King, M., and Young, P. (2001). Instructional program coherence: What is it and why it should guide school improvement policy? *Education Evaluation and Policy Analysis*, 23(4), 297–322.

Nichols, S., & Berliner, C. (2007) *Collateral damage*. Cambridge, Mass.: Harvard Education Press.

Obiakor, F. E. (2006). Valuing exceptional ethnic minority voices: New leadership for a new era. *Educational Considerations*, 34(1), 2.

Orr, M. T., Berg, B., Shore, R., & Meier, E. (2008). Putting the pieces together: Leadership for change in low-performing urban schools. *Education and Urban Society*, 40(6), 670–693.

Orr, T. (2006). Mapping innovation in leadership preparation in our nation's schools of Education. *Phi Delta Kappan*, 87(7), 492–500.

Owens R. (1995). *Organizational behavior in education*. Boston: Allyn & Bacon.

Papa, R., & Brown, R. (2007). On the founding of joint and independent doctoral programs in educational administration programs. *The Handbook of Doctoral Programs in Educational Administration: Issues and Challenges*. NCPEA Connexions e-book. www.connexions.soe.vt.edu/docbook.html.

Parkay, F., Hass, G., & Anctil, E. (2010) *Curriculum leadership* (9th ed.). Boston: Allyn & Bacon.

Peterson, K., and Deal, T. (2002). *Shaping school culture field book*. San Francisco: Jossey-Bass.

Peterson, K., and Finn, C. (1985). Principals, superintendents and administrator's art. *Public Interest*, 79, 42–62.

Quigney, T. (2008). The reauthorization of the no child left behind act: Recommended practices regarding teaching students with disabilities. *Planning and Changing*, 39(3&4), 146–158.

Ramirez, D., & Severn, L. (2006). Gap or Gaps: Challenging the singular definition of the achievement gap. *Education and Urban Society*, 39(1), 113–128.

Ramirez, A., Burnett, B., Meagher, S., Garcia, J., & Lewis, R. (2009). Preparing Future school leaders: How can it be accomplished online? In Achilles, C., Irby, B., Alford, B., & Perreaulty, G. (Eds.) *Remember our mission: Making Education and schools better for students. The 16th annual yearbook of the National Council of Professors of Educational Administration*. Lancaster, Pa.: DES Tech Publications, Inc., 59–71.

Razik, T., & Swanson, A. (2010). *Fundamental concepts of educational leadership and management*. Boston: Allyn & Bacon.

Rebore, R., & Walmsley, A. (2007). *An evidence based approach to the practice of educational leadership*. Boston; Pearson.

Reis-Louis, M. (2001). Surprise and sense making: What newcomers experience in entering unfamiliar organizational settings. In J. M. Shafritz & J. S. Ott (Eds.), *Classics of organizational theory* (5th ed.). Philadelphia: Harcourt , 377–390.

Rodriquez, G., & Fabionar, J. (2010). The impact of poverty on students and schools: Exploring the social justice leadership implications. In C. Marshall & M. Oliva (Eds.), *Leadership for social justice* (10–35). Boston: Allyn & Bacon.

Rodriquez, G., & Rolle, A. (2007). *To what ends and by what means? The social justice implications of contemporary school finance theory and policy*. New York: Routledge.

Rolle, A. (2004). *Peabody journal of education: Special issue on k-12 education finance—New directions for future research*. 79(3). Mahwah, N.J.: Lawrence Erlbaum, 10–35.

Rothstein, R. (2004). *Class and schools: Using social, economic, and educational reform to close the black-white gap*. New York: Teachers College Press.

Scheurich, J. (1998). Highly successful and loving public elementary school populated by low S.E.S. children of color: Core beliefs and cultural characteristics. *Urban Education*, 33(4), 451–491.

Scheurich, J., & Skrla, L. (2003). *Leadership for equity and excellence*. Thousand Oaks, Calif.: Corwin Press.

Schroth, G., & Pankake, A. (1999). A comparison of pedagogical approaches to teaching Graduate students in educational administration. *Journal of Instructional Psychology*, 26, 4–16.

Sergiovanni, T. (2006). *Rethinking leadership: A collection of articles*. Thousand Oaks, Calif.: Sage

Sherman, R., & Jones, T. (2008). Curriculum, instruction, and assessment. In J. Vornberg (Ed.), *Texas public school organization and administration*. Dubuque, Iowa: Kendall Hunt Publishers, 324–364.

Shidemantle, S., & Hoyle, J. (2004). Connecting superintendents with the technical core of teaching and learning: A synthesis of research findings. In C. Carr and C. Fullmer (Eds.) *Knowing the way, showing the way, and going the way. Eleventh yearbook of National Council of Professors of Educational Administration*. Lanham, Md.: Scarecrow Pub. 157-72.

Shields, C. M. (2004). Dialogic leadership for social justice: Overcoming pathologies of silence. *Educational Administration Quarterly*, 40(1), 109–132.

Simola, H. (1998). Firmly bolted into the air: Wishful rationalism as a discursive basis for educational reforms. *Teachers College Record*, 99(4), 731–757.

Singam, R. (2007, August-September). Training at the frontline, success at the bottom line: Employee training and education are the most reliable tools companies can use to keep an edge on competition. *Today's Manager*, 1–3.

Slattery, P., & Rapp, D. (2003). *Ethics and the foundations of education*. Boston: Pearson.

SLPPS (2009). *School leadership preparation and practice survey*. Salt Lake City: University of Utah Policy Center.

Spillane, J. (2007). *Distributive leadership in practice*. New York: Teachers College Press.

Spillane, J. P., Diamond, J. B., & Jita, L. (2003). Leading instruction: The distribution of leadership for instruction. *Journal of Curriculum Studies*, 35(5), 533–543.

Spring, J. (2002). *American education* (10th ed.). Boston: McGraw-Hill.

Strike, K. (2007). *Ethical leadership in schools.* Thousand Oaks, Calif.: Corwin Press.

Theoharis, G. (2007). Social justice educational leaders and resistance: Toward a theory of social justice leadership. *Educational Administration Quarterly,* 43(2), 221–258.

Thornton, G. (1992). *Assessment centers in human resource management.* New York: Addison-Wesley.

Torres, M. (2004). Best interests of students left behind? Exploring the ethical and legal dimensions of United States involvement in public school improvement. *Journal of Educational Administration,* 42(2), 249–269.

Torres, M., & Chen, Y. (2006). Assessing Columbine's impact on students' fourth amendment case outcomes: Implications for administrative discretion and decision making. *NASSP Bulletin,* 90(3), 185–206.

Torres, M., & Hoyle, J. (2008). Student' reflections of the relevance and quality of the relevance and quality of highly ranked doctoral programs in educational administration: Beacons of leadership preparation? *AASA Journal of Scholarship and Practice,* 5(2), 5–14.

Tortorici, M. A., Skledar, S. J., Zemaitis, M. A., Weber, R. J., Smith, R. B., Kroboth, P. D., & Poloyac, S. M. (2007). A model for supporting and training clinical pharmaceutical scientist PhD students. *American Journal of Pharmaceutical Education,* 71(2), 32.

Trowler, P. (1998). *Academics responding to change: new higher education frameworks and academic cultures.* Great Britain: Society for Research into Higher Education & Open University Press.

Ulrich, D., Zenger, J., & Smallwood, J. (1999). *Results-based leadership: How leaders build the business and improve the bottom line.* Boston: Harvard Press.

The University of Texas, Austin (n.d.). Principal program: Admissions requirements. Retrieved July 14, 2009, from edb.utexas.edu/education/departments/edadmin/programs/pselp/areas/principalship/admissions/requirements/.

The University of Wisconsin, Madison (n.d.). Educational leadership and policy analysis: Admission requirements and application procedures. Retrieved July 14, 2009, www.education.wisc.edu/elpa/admissions/general_adm.html.

U.S. News and World Report, America's best universities (March 2007), 1–14.

Vornberg, J. (2008). Systematic approach to educational accountability: Standards, programs, and procedures in Texas. In J. Vornberg (Ed.), *Texas public school organization and administration: 2008* (113–142). Dubuque, Iowa; Kendall Hunt.

Wallace Foundation. (2008). *Becoming a leader: Preparing principals for today's schools.* New York: Wallace Foundation Publishers.

Waters, J. T., & Marzano, R. (2006). *School district leadership that works: The effect of superintendent leadership on student achievement.* Denver: Mid-continent Research for Education and Learning.

Waters, T. (2007). Leadership responsibilities and student success? Invited Lecture, American Association of School Administrators Conference, 2007.

Waters, T., Marzano, R., & McNulty (2003). *School leadership that works.* Alexandria, VA: Association for Supervison and Curriculum Development.

Weick, K. D. (1976). Educational organizations as loosely coupled systems. *Administrative science quarterly,* 21, 1–19.

Weick, K. E. (1995). *Sensemaking in organizations*. Thousand Oaks, Calif.: Sage.

Wickersham, L. (2008). Texas schools, technology integration, and the twenty-first century. In J. Vornberg (Ed.), Texas public school organization and administration: 2008. Dubuque, Iowa: Kendall-Hunt, 611–627.

Wilmore, E. (2002a). *Principal leadership*. Thousand Oaks, Calif.: Corwin Press.

———. (2002b). *The principalship: Applying the new educational leadership constituent council (ELLC) standards*. Thousand Oaks, Calif.: Corwin Press.

Wong, K., & Nicotera, A. (2007). *Successful schools and educational accountability*. Boston: Pearson.

Woo, J. (1986). Graduate degrees and job success: Managers in one U.S. corporation. *Economics of Education Review*, 5(3), 227–237.

Yeh, S. (2006). Can rapid assessment moderate the consequences of high-stakes testing? *Education and Urban Society*, 39(1), 91–112.

Young, M., Creighton, T., Crow, G., Orr, T., & Ogawa, R. (2005, May). *An educative look at educating school leaders*. Austin, Tex.: University Council for Educational Administration, National Council of Professors of Educational Administration, and Division A of the American Association of Educational Research Association.

Zimmerman, J., Bowman, J., Valentine, M., and Barnes, R. (2004). The principal cohort leadership academy: A partnership that connects theory and practice. In C. Carr, & C. Fulmer (Eds.), *The Twelfth Annual Yearbook of the National Council of Professors of Educational Administration* (224–240). Lanham, Md.: Scarecrow Publishers.

Index

Breinigsville, PA USA
24 March 2010

234858BV00001B/5/P

9 781607 096870